First World War
and Army of Occupation
War Diary
France, Belgium and Germany

47 DIVISION
140 Infantry Brigade
London Regiment
8th (City of London) Battalion (Post Office Rifles)
1 January 1916 - 31 July 1916

WO95/2731/3

The Naval & Military Press Ltd
www.nmarchive.com
Published in association with The National Archives

Published by

The Naval & Military Press Ltd

Unit 10 Ridgewood Industrial Park,

Uckfield, East Sussex,

TN22 5QE England

Tel: +44 (0) 1825 749494

www.naval-military-press.com

www.nmarchive.com

This diary has been reprinted in facsimile from the original. Any imperfections are inevitably reproduced and the quality may fall short of modern type and cartographic standards.

© **Crown Copyright**
Images reproduced by permission of The National Archives, London, England, 2015.

Contents

Document type	Place/Title	Date From	Date To
Heading	1/8 London Regt Jan Vol XI		
War Diary	Trenches D2	01/01/1916	02/01/1916
War Diary	Verquin	03/01/1916	03/01/1916
War Diary	Les Brebis	04/01/1916	04/01/1916
War Diary	Maroc	05/01/1916	07/01/1916
War Diary	Braquemont	08/01/1916	11/01/1916
War Diary	Loos	12/01/1916	12/01/1916
War Diary	Loos	13/01/1916	19/01/1916
War Diary	Les Brebis	20/01/1916	23/01/1916
War Diary	Maroc	24/01/1916	31/01/1916
Miscellaneous	140th Infantry Brigade.	05/01/1916	05/01/1916
Miscellaneous	140th Infantry Brigade.		
Operation(al) Order(s)	140th Infantry Brigade Operation Order No. 63.	04/01/1916	04/01/1916
Operation(al) Order(s)	140th Infantry Brigade. Operation Order No. 52	04/01/1916	04/01/1916
Operation(al) Order(s)	140th Infantry Brigade Operation Order No.49.	01/01/1916	01/01/1916
Miscellaneous	A Form. Messages And Signals.		
Operation(al) Order(s)	140th Infantry Brigade Operation Order No. 50.		
Miscellaneous	March Table To 140th Infantry Brigade Operation Order No. 50.		
Operation(al) Order(s)	140th Infantry Brigade Operation Order No. 51.	03/01/1916	03/01/1916
Miscellaneous	140th Infantry Brigade March Table To Accompany Operation Order No. 51.		
Operation(al) Order(s)	140th Infantry Brigade Operation Order No. 54.	07/01/1916	07/01/1916
Miscellaneous	140th Infantry Brigade Table To Accompany Operation Order No. 54.		
Operation(al) Order(s)	140th Infantry Brigade Operation Order No. 55.	10/01/1916	10/01/1916
Miscellaneous	140th Infantry Brigade Table To Accompany Operation Order No. 55.		
Operation(al) Order(s)	148th Infantry Brigade Operation Order No. 56.	14/01/1916	14/01/1916
Miscellaneous			
Operation(al) Order(s)	140th Infantry Brigade Operation Order No. 57.	19/01/1916	19/01/1916
Miscellaneous			
Miscellaneous	140th Infantry Brigade Table To Accompany Operation Order No. 57.		
Miscellaneous	140th Infantry Brigade Operation Order No. 58.	22/01/1916	22/01/1916
Miscellaneous	140th Infantry Brigade Table To Accompany Operation Order No. 58.		
Miscellaneous	140th Infantry Brigade. Operation Order No. 59.	31/01/1916	31/01/1916
Miscellaneous	Relief Table Issued With Operation Order No. 59.		
War Diary	South Maroc Noeux-Les-Mirer (Braquemont)	01/02/1916	01/02/1916
War Diary	Noeux-Les-Mines (Braquemont)	02/02/1916	04/02/1916
War Diary	Loos	05/02/1916	13/02/1916
War Diary	Loos Les Brebis	14/02/1916	14/02/1916
War Diary	Les Brebis Lillers	15/02/1916	15/02/1916
War Diary	Lillers	16/02/1916	28/02/1916
War Diary	Lillers	29/02/1916	29/02/1916
Miscellaneous			
Operation(al) Order(s)	140th Infantry Brigade Operation Order No. 60	04/02/1916	04/02/1916
Miscellaneous	140th Infantry Brigade Schedule To Accompany Operation Order No. 60.		

Type	Description	Date From	Date To
Operation(al) Order(s)	140th Infantry Brigade Operation Order No. 61.	08/02/1916	08/02/1916
Miscellaneous	140th Infantry Brigade.	10/02/1916	10/02/1916
Miscellaneous	8th Bn. London Regiment.	01/01/1916	01/01/1916
Operation(al) Order(s)	140th Infantry Brigade. Operation Order No. 62.	12/02/1916	12/02/1916
Miscellaneous			
Miscellaneous	140th Infantry Brigade. Appendix I.		
Miscellaneous	140th Infantry Brigade Appendix II		
Miscellaneous	8th Bn. London Regiment.	18/02/1916	18/02/1916
Operation(al) Order(s)	140th Infantry Brigade. Operation Order No. 63.	28/02/1916	28/02/1916
Miscellaneous	Programme Of Move Of 47th Division From 1st Army.		
Miscellaneous			
Miscellaneous	Table "D"-47th Division.		
Miscellaneous	Unit Serial Description.	12/02/1916	12/02/1916
Miscellaneous		15/02/1916	15/02/1916
Miscellaneous	47th (London) Division.	15/02/1916	15/02/1916
Miscellaneous	47th (London) Division.		
Miscellaneous	Headquarters. 140th Infantry Brigade.	18/02/1916	18/02/1916
Miscellaneous	Officer Commanding. 8th Bn. London Regiment.	18/02/1916	18/02/1916
Map	Vertical And Oblique Photographs & Portion Of Sheet Area Covered.		
War Diary	Bomy	01/03/1916	03/03/1916
War Diary	Redinghem	04/03/1916	08/03/1916
War Diary	Fiefs	09/03/1916	09/03/1916
War Diary	Ourton	10/03/1916	15/03/1916
War Diary	Gouy-Servins	16/03/1916	21/03/1916
War Diary	Trenches	22/03/1916	26/03/1916
War Diary	Estree-Cauchie	27/03/1916	31/03/1916
Miscellaneous	140th Infantry Brigade Order No. 65.	08/03/1916	08/03/1916
Miscellaneous	March Table.		
Operation(al) Order(s)	140th Infantry Brigade Order No. 66.	09/03/1916	09/03/1916
Miscellaneous	March Table.		
Miscellaneous	4th Corps No.R.S.NR610.	05/03/1916	05/03/1916
Miscellaneous	London Regt.		
Miscellaneous			
Miscellaneous	Recently published By The Commander-in Chief	17/03/1916	17/03/1916
Miscellaneous	Schedule.		
Operation(al) Order(s)	140th Infantry Brigade Order No. 69.	25/03/1916	25/03/1916
Operation(al) Order(s)	140th Infantry Brigade Order No. 67.		
Miscellaneous	Table Of Moves.		
Operation(al) Order(s)	140th Infantry Brigade Order No. 68.	19/03/1916	19/03/1916
Operation(al) Order(s)	140th Brigade Order No. 70.	31/03/1916	31/03/1916
Miscellaneous	Schedule.		
Miscellaneous	March Table.		
Miscellaneous	140th Infantry Brigade.	06/03/1916	06/03/1916
Miscellaneous	Sketch Shewing Dumps		
Operation(al) Order(s)	Operation Order No. 7		
Miscellaneous	A Form. Messages And Signals.		
Miscellaneous	Headquarters, 140th Infantry Brigade.		
Miscellaneous	140th Infantry Brigade Order No. 64.	03/03/1916	03/03/1916
Miscellaneous	Schedule		
Miscellaneous	140th Infantry Brigade.	07/03/1916	07/03/1916
Miscellaneous	8 London Regt. Vol XIV April 1916		
Miscellaneous	IVth Corps. No. H.R.S.624. First Army No. G.S. 344	16/04/1916	16/04/1916
War Diary	Estree Cauchie	01/04/1916	01/04/1916
War Diary	Gouy-Servins	02/04/1916	07/04/1916
War Diary	Villers au-Bois A Sub Section Cartnoy Sector	08/04/1916	13/04/1916

War Diary	Verdrel	14/04/1916	18/04/1916
War Diary	Bouvigny Huts	19/04/1916	19/04/1916
War Diary	Lorette Trenches	20/04/1916	25/04/1916
War Diary	Villers Au Bois Carency	26/04/1916	30/04/1916
Miscellaneous			
Miscellaneous	IVth Corps No. S/1 (I).	05/04/1916	05/04/1916
Miscellaneous	Schedule.		
Miscellaneous			
Operation(al) Order(s)	140th Infantry Brigade Order No. 71.	06/04/1916	06/04/1916
Miscellaneous	A Form. Messages And Signals.		
Operation(al) Order(s)	140th Infantry Brigade Order No. 72.	12/04/1916	12/04/1916
Miscellaneous	Schedule.		
Operation(al) Order(s)	140th Infantry Brigade Order No. 73.	18/04/1916	18/04/1916
Miscellaneous	Schedule.		
Miscellaneous	A Form. Messages And Signals.		
Operation(al) Order(s)	140th Infantry Brigade Order No. 74.	24/04/1916	24/04/1916
Miscellaneous	Schedule.		
Miscellaneous	Operation Order No. 6 By Captain W.B. Vince. 8th April 1916	08/04/1916	08/04/1916
Operation(al) Order(s)	Operation Order No.8 by Lt. Col: A. Maxwell	20/04/1916	20/04/1916
Operation(al) Order(s)	Operation Order No. 8	20/04/1916	20/04/1916
Miscellaneous	8th Battn. London Regt.	30/04/1916	30/04/1916
Miscellaneous	47th (London) Division. Programme Of Infantry Reliefs For May 1916.	28/04/1916	28/04/1916
Miscellaneous	140th Infantry Brigade Order No. 75.	30/04/1916	30/04/1916
Miscellaneous	Schedule.		
Miscellaneous	140th Infantry Brigade Order No. 76.	06/05/1916	06/05/1916
Miscellaneous	Schedule.		
Operation(al) Order(s)	Operation Order No 10	18/05/1916	18/05/1916
Operation(al) Order(s)	140th Infantry Brigade Order No. 80.	24/05/1916	24/05/1916
Miscellaneous	March Table.		
Operation(al) Order(s)	140th Infantry Brigade. Operation Order No. 77.	10/05/1916	10/05/1916
Miscellaneous	Officer Commanding.	22/06/1916	22/06/1916
Heading	140th Brigade. 47th Division. 1/8th. Battalion London Regiment July 1916		
War Diary		01/07/1916	12/07/1916
Miscellaneous			
War Diary		14/07/1916	31/07/1916
Operation(al) Order(s)	Operation Order No. 16	01/07/1916	01/07/1916
Operation(al) Order(s)	Operation Order No 7 By Major W.J Whitewood OC 8th Regt.	04/07/1916	04/07/1916
Operation(al) Order(s)	Operation Order No 7	07/07/1916	07/07/1916
Operation(al) Order(s)	Operation Order No. 18 by Major W.G. Whitehead O.C. 8th Battalion London Regt.	15/07/1916	15/07/1916
Miscellaneous			
Operation(al) Order(s)	Operation Order No. 19 By Major W.J. Whitehead Commanding 84th Bn London Rgt (P.O.R.)	21/07/1916	21/07/1916
Operation(al) Order(s)	Operation Order No. 20 By Lt. Col W.J. Whitehead Commdg 84th Bn London Regt (P.O.R.)	25/07/1916	25/07/1916
Miscellaneous	Code Word		
Miscellaneous	A Form. Messages And Signals		

1/9 Kurdwon Regt
Jain
Vol XI

Army Form C. 2118

8th London Regiment
(Post Office Rifles)

WAR DIARY
INTELLIGENCE SUMMARY

January 1916.

Place	Date	Hour	Summary of Events and Information	Remarks and references to Appendices
Trenches D2	Jan 1	—	Bn. remained in support in D2. Following mentioned in Despatches:– Lt. Col. Harvey D.S.O., Major Whiteland, Capt T.H.P. Morris, Lt. B.A. Moor (since d. of wounds), Lt. A. Peel, Lt. R.A. Thomas, 2 Lt. O.J. Lawrence (killed); 1493 A/Sgt. Heather W., 212 Sgt. Tapfield C.R. (killed); 1298 Pt. Clark W.	
"	2	—	Bn. relieved 13th London Regt. in the front line D2, relief commencing 6.30 p.m. 2 a.m. — OR, 1 killed, 1 wounded.	
"	3	—	Bn. relieved in morning by 2nd Dismounted Br., marching by "Coy. & standing by 1 Coy. A. B. D. Gs. after reliefs, A/B moved to VERQUIN & went into billets there.	
Verquin	4	—	Bn. left Verquin at 3.30 and marched to Les Brebis & went into billets.	
Les Brebis	5	—	Starting at 7.30 p.m. Bn. relieved parts of French 32nd & 66th Regiments in N. and S. Maroc, the Brigade taking over the new Maroc Sector from the French, and the Bn. being in Brigade Reserve.	
Maroc	6–7	—	Bn. remained in support in Maroc sector — OR 65, 3 OR. wounded.	
"	8	—	Bn. was relieved by 23rd London Regt.'s relief commencing 6 p.m. After relief Bn. marched to Les Brebis and proceeded from there in lorries to Braquemont (Noeux-les-Mines) where it went into billets; the brigade going into Divisional Reserve.	
Braquemont	9–11	—	Bn. remained in billets.	
Loos	12	—	Bn. left billets at 4 p.m. and marched via [...] Les Brebis to relieve 17th London Regt. in Right Sub-	

8th London Regiment
(Post Office Rifles)

WAR DIARY
INTELLIGENCE SUMMARY

January 1916 (cont.)

Army Form C. 2118

Place	Date	Hour	Summary of Events and Information	Remarks and references to Appendices
Loos	Jan 13-14	-	Bn. remained in Right sub section, Loos Sector. Following Honours gazetted on 14th :- Military Cross, Major T.H.R. Harris, 2nd Lieut H. Peel; D.C.M., No. 1699 A/Sgt. J.W. Rushforth, No. 2532 Pte H. Perree, No. 2026 Pte W.J. Varney.	
"	15	-	On night of 15th-16th the line was readjusted and the Bn sub section became the Centre sub section of Adjusted Loos Sector. 1 OR wounded.	
"	16-19	-	Bn remained in that sub section on following:- 16th, 1 OR wounded; 17th, 1 OR wounded; 18th 1 OR killed, 3 OR wounded; 19th, 1 OR killed.	
Les Brebis	20	-	Bn was relieved by 2nd London Regt, relief commenced about 6 p.m. & went to billets at Les Brebis where it was placed at disposal of G.O.C. Maroc Section as Bde Reserve.	
"	21-23	-	Bn. remains in billets at Les Brebis.	
"	24	-	Bn relieved 19th London Regt in support in Maroc left [sub] sector; HQrs & 2 Coys in A Maroc, 2 Coys in N Maroc. No casualties.	
Maroc	25-28	-	Bn. remained in support in Maroc sector, time employed through being made in supervision. Casualties 26th – 2 OR killed, 1 OR wounded; 28th, 1 OR wounded.	
"	29	-	Bn relieved 7th London Regt in B sub section, Maroc Sector.	
"	30-31	-	Bn remained in B sub sector, Maroc sector, 31st, 1 OR killed, 2 OR wounded.	

[signature] Lt. Col.
Ot. 8t London Regt (P.O.R.)

2 February 1916.

SECRET.   BM/422

140th INFANTRY BRIGADE.

5th January, 1916.

Reference – Operation Order No. 52, para: 8, issued 4th January, 1916.

Reference Map – New blue print issued to units by G.O.C. on night of
4th/5th January, 1916.

1. The Brigade front will extend from N.9.d.3.7 to M.5.b.2.5.

2. Movements of units will be in accordance with attached Table.

3. 225 rounds of S.A.A., to be drawn from Regimental supplies, will be carried per man.

4. Brigade Ammunition Store will be in house at M.2.b.2.2.
   Quartermasters' Stores will remain at LES BREBIS.

5. First line transport will remain at LES BREBIS.

6. Gum boots and steel helmets will be issued to units at 10 a.m. today.

7. Two days rations will be carried if practicable; otherwise Battalions must arrange for carrying up their own rations.

8. The Brigade will be relieved by the 142nd Infantry Brigade on the evening of the 7th instant.

9. Brigade Headquarters will move from LES BREBIS to Headquarters of 35th French Brigade, opposite Brewery in BULLY GRENAY, about R.10.b.5.6, Reference Map 36B 1/40000, at 8 a.m. on 6th January, 1916.

                                                       Captain,
                               Acting Brigade Major,
                               140th Infantry Brigade.

Copy No.		
1	Operation Orders File	
2	War Diary	
3	47th Division	By Signal Section.
4	4th Bn. London Regt.	,,
5	6th ,,	,,
6	7th ,,	,,
7	8th ,,	,,
8	15th ,,	,,
9	47/1 Light Mortar Bty.	,,
10	No. 7 T.M. Battery	,,
11	Bde. Machine Gun Coy.	,,
12	Bde. Grenadier Coy.	,,
13	O.C., Bde. Ammn. Reserve	,,

173

140th INFANTRY BRIGADE.

Unit	Limits of Sub-sections	Bn. Headquarters	Time for units to meet guides	Guides	Remarks
6th Bn. London Regiment	M.9.d.3.7 to M.9.b.3.4	To be communicated later.	7.30 p.m.	As arranged between Commanding Officers of relieving & relieved units.	
7th do.	M.9.b.3.4 to M.4.a.0.0	do.	6.30 p.m.		
15th do.	M.4.a.0.0 to M.4.b.5.3	do.	6.0 p.m.		
6th do.	M.4.b.5.3 to M.5.b.2.5	do.	5.30 p.m.		
8th do.	M.Grs. & 2 Companies in Sth. Maroc. 2 Companies in Old British line M.3.b.9.1 to M.3.b.8.9.	do.	7.30 p.m.		
47/1 Light Mortar Battery	From Western point of North-arm of DOUBLE CRASSIER to left of Section (M.5.b.2.5)	do.	5.30 p.m.		Positions to be taken up not later than 6 a.m. on 6/7/16.
No. 7 Trench Mortar Battery	From right of Section M.9.d.3.7 to Western extremity of DOUBLE CRASSIER	do.	4.30 p.m.		
Brigade Machine Gun Coy.	In positions to be selected by O.C. Company.	do.			
Brigade Grenadier Coy.	In groups as arranged by the Brigade Grenadier Officer.	do.	As arranged by Brigade Grenadier Officer.		

SECRET.

Copy No. 7

140th INFANTRY BRIGADE
OPERATION ORDER No. 53.

IN THE FIELD
4th January, 1916.

1. During the period in which the Brigade remains at LES BREBIS before moving into the line, the 6th and 7th Battalions will be placed at the disposal of G.O.C., 18th French Division as support to the left (LOOS) sector.

2. In case of attack:-
   (a) The 6th Battalion proceeds through MAROC to the old German and British trenches as follows:-
   2 Coys. in Old German trenches - Right Coy. astride of the BOYAU DU TOIT and the left Coy. astride of the BOYAU DU CENTRE, its left in the neighbourhood of the POSTE DE COMMANDEMENT of the O. .C., 36th Brigade.
   2 Coys. in old British trenches - Right Coy. astride of BOYAU DU TOIT and the left Coy. astride of the BOYAU DU CENTRE.
   (b) The 7th Battalion will proceed to N. MAROC passing N. of GRENAY using the communication trench of No. 2 position - formerly known as FINCHLEY ROAD - or moving over the open in Artillery Formation. This Battn. will occupy positions as follows:-
   2 Coys. in bomb-proof shelters - one in TRAIT d'UNION trench and the second in VERSAILLES trench.
   1 Coy. in Old German trenches between P. de C. of Brigade Commander and BETHUNE road.
   1 Coy. in Old British trench astride of BOYAU DU NORD.
   (c) Battalion Commanders will report arrival of their Battns. to O. .C. 36th Inf.Bde. (French) and through him to Divisional Headquarters.
   O.C's., both Battalions will remain with G.O.C. 36th Inf Bde. and will receive their orders from the Division through him.

3. The 4th, 8th and 15th Battalions and M.G.Coy. will remain at disposal of G.O.C. 140th Infantry Brigade.

4. All units will be at one hour's notice and on the alarm being given, M.G.Coy. and 1st Line Transport will harness up and hook in.

5. O.C's 6th and 7th Battalions will reconnoitre their positions tomorrow.

6. Bde. Report Centre will be at the present Headquarters in HIGH BUILDING.

T B Brady
Captain,
Acting Brigade Major,
140th Infantry Brigade.

Copy No. 1 Op.Orders File.
"   2 War Diary.
"   3 47th Divn.   By. Sig.Sec.   Copy No. 8 6th Batt.   By Sig.Sec.
"   4 G.O.C.,18th French Divn.   "   9 15th "   "
"   5 4th Batt.   By Sig. Sec.   "   10 M.G.Coy.   "
"   6 6th "   "
"   7 7th "

175

SECRET.

Copy No. 7

140th INFANTRY BRIGADE.

OPERATION ORDER No. 52.

4th January, 1916.

1. The Brigade will take over the MAROC Section of trenches on night of 5th/6th January, 1916, from the 85th French Brigade.

2. The General Officer Commanding desires to see all Battalion Commanders accompanied by their Adjutants, Officer Commanding Brigade Grenadier Company, Officer Commanding Machine Gun Company, and Captain GAZE, 18th Bn. London Regiment, at 9 p.m. tonight at Brigade Headquarters' Mess Room, LES BREBIS, when maps will be issued and front to be held by each Battalion indicated.

3. Five guides from 85th French Brigade will meet the Commanding Officer and 4 Company Officers of each Battalion at 7 a.m. on 5th January, 1916, at place to be communicated, vide para: 2, and conduct them to Headquarters of Officer Commanding French Battalion to be relieved.

4. On completion of reconnaissance of trenches, Battalion Commanders will arrange with Officer Commanding French unit being relieved for guides to meet relieving Battalion at 5.30 p.m. on night of 5th/6th January, 1916, at place to be mutually arranged.

5. Officer Commanding Brigade Machine Gun Company will meet Officer of 68th French Regiment at same time and place as Battalion Officers (vide para: 3) for reconnaissance of machine gun positions.

6. Officer Commanding Brigade Signal Company will report to Etat Major at Headquarters of 85th French Brigade at BULLY GRENAY at 7 a.m. on 5th January, 1916.

7. Officer Commanding Brigade Grenadier Company will send parties to dumps as early as practicable on morning of 5th January, 1916, to fuse grenades.

8. Further detailed instructions in reference to relief will be issued later.

F.B.Brady.

Captain,
Acting Brigade Major,
140th Infantry Brigade.

Copy No. 1	Op.Order File		Copy No. 7	8th Batt.	Sig.Sec
,, 2	War Diary		,, 8	15th ,,	,,
,, 3	47th Divn.	By Signal Section.	,, 9	B.M.G.Co.	,,
,, 4	4th Batt.	,,	,, 10	B.G.Offr.	,,
,, 5	6th ,,	,,	,, 11	Capt.GAZE	,,
,, 6	7th ,,	,,	,, 12	O.C.Bde.Sig.Coy.	

SECRET.   Copy No. 7

140th INFANTRY BRIGADE

OPERATION ORDER No. 49.

                                                    1st January, 1918.

1. The 8th Bn. London Regiment will relieve the 1st Bn. in D.2 on 2nd January, 1918. Relief to commence at 7.30 a.m. On relief, 15th Bn. London Regiment will come into support.
    The 7th Bn. London Regiment will relieve 6th Bn. London Regiment in D.1 on morning of 2nd January, 1918. Relief to commence at 8 a.m. On relief, 6th Bn. London Regiment will take over billets of 7th Bn. London Regiment at CAILLY LABOURSE.

2. Lewis guns in each sub-section will commence relief at 7 a.m.

3. Guides will be arranged between Officers Commanding Battalions concerned.

4. The 8th and 7th Bns. London Regiment will take 24 hours complete rations into the trenches with them.

5. The Brigade will be relieved on morning of 3rd January, 1918, and will probably be billeted in VERQUIN on night of 3rd/4th January, 1918.

                                            [signature]
                                            Captain,
                                            for Brigade Major,
                                            140th Infantry Brigade.

Copy No.	1	Operation Orders File.	
"	2	War Diary.	
"	3	47th Division.	By Signal Section.
"	4	4th Bn. London Regiment.	"
"	5	6th "	"
"	6	7th "	"
"	7	8th "	"
"	8	15th "	"
"	9	Brigade Grenadier Officer	"
"	10	47/1 Light Mortar Battery	"
"	11	142nd Infy. Brigade.	"
"	12	19th "	"
"	13	Brigade Machine Gun Coy.	"
"	14	No.8 Trench Mortar Battery	"

179

"A" Form.
MESSAGES AND SIGNALS.

Army Form C. 2121.

| Office of Origin and Service Instructions: 2NZ | Words: 26 Sent At To By | This message is on a/c of: OD Service. (Signature of "Franking Officer.") | Recd. at 11.10 p.m. Date 4/4/15 From 2 NZ By A/Cpl Martin |

TO: 7TH LON REGT

| Sender's Number: BM/182 | Day of Month: Two | In reply to Number: | AAA |

In operation order no. 50 para. 3 issued tonight please read BREWERY CORNER for CLARKES KEEP

From Place: 140TH INF BDE
Time: 9.50 pm

Copy No. 7

SECRET.

140th INFANTRY BRIGADE

OPERATION ORDER No. 50.

1. The 140th Infantry Brigade will be relieved in Section "D" by the 1st Dismounted Brigade on the morning of 3rd January, 1916.

2. Movements will be according to attached Table.

3. All trench stores (including maps and defence schemes) will be handed over, except gum boots and steel helmets. Consolidated lists will be sent to this Office.
Gum boots will be taken off at ~~CLARKE'S KEEP~~ BREWERY CORNER and put on motor lorries for removal. IT IS ESSENTIAL THAT BOOTS BE STRAPPED TOGETHER IN PAIRS.

4. The completion of reliefs will be reported to Brigade Headquarters at CHATEAU DES PRES.

5. On completion of relief, Brigade Headquarters will move to CHATEAU at VERQUIN.

6. On 4th January, 1916, the Brigade will move to billets in LES BREBIS. Further orders will be issued.

7. Transport will move with Battalions.

J.B.Brady

ack. Captain,
for Brigade Major,
140th Infantry Brigade.

Copy No. 1	Operation Orders File.	
,, 2	War Diary.	
,, 3	47th Division.	By Signal Section.
,, 4	4th Bn. London Regt.	,,
,, 5	6th ,,	,,
,, 6	7th ,,	,,
,, 7	8th ,,	,,
,, 8	15th ,,	,,
,, 9	Brigade Machine Gun Company.	,,
,, 10	Brigade Grenadier Officer.	,,
,, 11	47/1 Light Mortar Battery	,,
,, 12	No. 8 Trench Mortar Btty.	,,
,, 13	1st Dismounted Brigade.	,,
,, 14	19th Infantry Brigade	,,
,, 15	142nd ,,	,,

MARCH TABLE TO 140th INFANTRY BRIGADE OPERATION ORDER No. 50.

Date	Unit of 140 Infy. Bde.	In	Relieved by	Guides	Billeting area on relief	Route	Remarks
1916 3rd Jan.	7th Bn. London Regt.	D.1	2 Companies, 1st Dismounted Bn.	BREWERY CORNER, VERMELLES, at 7.30 a.m.	VERQUIN	Via Cross Roads in L.3.b and NOEUX-LES-MINES Stn.	To move by Companies after crossing railway in L.2.d.
,,	8th Bn. London Regt.	D.2	2 Companies, 2nd Dismounted Bn.	BREWERY CORNER, VERMELLES, at 8 a.m.	,,	do.	do.
,,	15th Bn. London Regt.	Support	1 Company, 1st Dismounted Bn.; 1 Company, 2nd Dismounted Bn.	BREWERY CORNER, VERMELLES, at 8.30 a.m.	HOUCHIN	do.	do.
,,	6th Bn. London Regt.	Reserve			,,	passing Cross Roads at L.3.b at 9 a.m.	do.
,,	4th Bn. London Regt.	,,			DROUVIN	passing Cross Roads L.3.b at 9.40 a.m.	do.
,,	47/1 Light Mortar Bty.	D.1 and D.2	1st Dismounted Bde. L.M.B.	Previously arranged.	HOUCHIN	Via Cross Roads in L.3.b and NOEUX-LES-MINES Stn.	To hand over positions at 7 a.m. and leave trenches at once.
,, (evening)	No.8 Trench Mortar Bty.	,,	No.68 Trench Mortar Bty. (1½")	To be notified later.	VERMELLES		
3rd Jan.	Machine Gun Company.				VERQUIN	do.	Arrangements to be made between Machine Gun Officers concerned.
,,	Bde. Grndr. Company.	D.1 and D.2	1st Dismounted Bde. Grndrs.	As arranged between Grndr. Offrs.	HOUCHIN	do.	

182

SECRET.

91.

Copy No.

140th INFANTRY BRIGADE.

OPERATION ORDER No. 51.

3rd January, 1916.

Reference   Map 1/40000, Sheet 36N.

1. The Brigade will move to LES BREBIS on Tuesday 4th January, 1916.

2. Units will move according to attached Table, and will pass the starting point (level crossing in L.14.c) at the hours mentioned.

3. Billeting parties will meet the Staff Captain at LES BREBIS Church at 2 p.m.

4. First Line Transport will accompany units.
   Brigade Headquarters will close at 3 p.m. and reopen on arrival at House in Church Square, LES BREBIS North of Church at L.35.b.0.7.

Issued at   p.m.

J.O.Brady,
Captain,
Acting Brigade Major,
140th Infantry Brigade.

Copy No.	1	Operation Orders File.	
,,	2	War Diary.	
,,	3	47th Division.	By Signal Section.
,,	4	4th Bn. London Regt.	,,
,,	5	6th ,,	,,
,,	6	7th ,,	,,
,,	7	8th ,,	,,
,,	8	15th ,,	,,
,,	9	Machine Gun Company	,,
,,	10	Brigade Grenadier Officer	,,
,,	11	47/1 Light Mortar Battery	,,

140th INFANTRY BRIGADE

MARCH TABLE TO ACCOMPANY OPERATION ORDER NO. 51.

Unit	Starting Point	Time	Route
7th Bn. London Regiment	Level Crossing L.14.c.	3.0 p.m.	Via BOKU-LES-MINES and MAZINGARBE.
8th do.	do.	3.10 p.m.	do.
15th do.	do.	3.20 p.m.	do.
6th do.	do.	3.30 p.m.	do.
4th do.	do.	3.40 p.m.	do.
47/1-Light Mortar Battery	do.	To march with 15th Bn. London Regiment	do.
Machine Gun Company	do.	3.50 p.m.	do.
Brigade Grenadier Company	do.	4.0 p.m.	do.
Brigade Headquarters	do.	3.50 p.m.	do.

SECRET.

140th INFANTRY BRIGADE

OPERATION ORDER No. 54.

7th January, 1916.

Reference Map - Secret Blue Print.

1. The 140th Infantry Brigade, less the 4th Bn. London Regiment, will be relieved by the 142nd Infantry Brigade in MAROC Section on night of Saturday, 8th/9th January, 1916.

2. The Brigade, on relief, will become Divisional Reserve.

3. The 7th Bn. London Regiment to be at call of General Officer Commanding MAROC Section, and the 6th Bn. London Regiment at call of General Officer Commanding LOOS Section, as Brigade Reserves if required tactically. These units will be at 1 hour's notice.

4. The 4th Bn. London Regiment will remain in the line, and come under the orders of the General Officer Commanding 142nd Infantry Brigade on completion of relief.

5. The Battalion sharpshooters now in the line, will remain in their present positions until 9 a.m. on the 9th instant, in order to familiarise sharpshooters of the 142nd Infantry Brigade with the new area.

6. Reliefs will take place in accordance with attached Table, and instructions as there shown will be communicated to their Lewis Gun Sections and Sharpshooters by Battalions concerned.

7. No. 7 Trench Mortar Battery will remain in the line.

8. Steel helmets will be handed over as Trench Stores to incoming units.
Gum boots are to be treated as Battalion Stores and brought out on relief.

9. Consolidated lists of Trench Stores handed over will be forwarded to Brigade Headquarters by 5 p.m. on the 9th inst.

10. Brigade Headquarters will move at 10 a.m. on 8th January 1916, to LES BREBIS (L.35.a.3.6, Sheet 36B 1/40000).

Issued at   p.m.

J.B.Brady
Captain,
Acting Brigade Major,
140th Infantry Brigade.

Copy No.	1	Operation Orders File.	
,,	2	War Diary.	
,,	3	47th Division	By Signal Section.
,,	4	4th Bn. London Regt.	,,
,,	5	6th do.	,,
,,	6	7th do.	,,
,,	7	8th do.	,,
,,	8	15th do.	,,
,,	9	Machine Gun Company.	,,
,,	10	Brigade Grndr. Officer	,,
,,	11	47/1 Light Mortar Bty.	,,
,,	12	No. 7 Trench Mortar Bty.	,,
,,	13	141st Infy. Brigade	,,
,,	14	142nd do.	,,

140th INFANTRY BRIGADE

TABLE TO ACCOMPANY OPERATION ORDER No. 54.

Relieving Unit	Unit to be relieved	In Sub-section	Time for guides to meet units	Meeting place for guides	Billets on relief	Route
21st Bn. London Regt.	6th Bn. London Regt.	D	4.30 p.m.	Iron Gate at point where EDGWARE ROAD TRENCH crosses HARROW ROAD. M.2.a.5.0 on blue print map.	LES BREBIS	To be arranged between units concerned.
23rd do.	8th do.	S Support	5.0 p.m.		NOEUX-LES-MINES	
22nd do.	7th do.	B	5.30 p.m.		H.Q's & 2 Coys. in LES BREBIS. 2 Coys. in STH. MAROC	
24th do.	15th do.	C	6.0 p.m.		LES BREBIS	
47/3 Light Mortar Bty.	47/1 Light Mortar By.	C & D	2.30 p.m.		LES BREBIS	
142nd Bde. Grndr. Coy.	140th Bde.Grndr.Coy.	A,B,C,D.	1.15 p.m.		With respective Battalions.	
142nd Bde. M.G. Coy.	140th Bde. M.G. Coy.	A,B,C,D.	1.30 p.m.		LES BREBIS	
142nd Bde. Lewis Gun Sections	140th Bde Lewis gun Sections.	A,B,C,D.	As given for their respective Bns.		With respective Battalions	
142nd Bde. Sharp-shooters	140th Bde. Sharp-shooters	A,B,C,D.	2.45 p.m.		With respective Battalions.	

SECRET.

Copy No. 7

140th INFANTRY BRIGADE
OPERATION ORDER No. 55.

10th January, 1916.

Map Reference - Secret Blue Print 1/10000.

1. The 140th Infantry Brigade, less the 4th Bn. London Regiment, will relieve the 141st Infantry Brigade in the LOOS Sector on the night of 12th/13th January, 1916.

2. Units will move into Sub-sectors in accordance with attached Table.

3. Lewis Gun Sections will move in after the relief of all Battalions is complete.

4. Sharpshooters and Grenadier Platoons will march with their Battalions.
Grenadiers will carry any short rifles available in their Battalions for firing rifle grenades.

5. One Section of 140th Brigade Machine Gun Company will relieve the Section of the 141st Brigade Machine Gun Company, now at the disposal of the 4th Bn. Royal Welsh Fusiliers for the defence of LOOS. Officer Commanding Machine Gun Company will make all arrangements.

6. Steel helmets of relieved units will be taken over on relief.

7. Brigade Headquarters will remain at LES BREBIS.

J.B. Brady
Captain,
Acting Brigade Major,
140th Infantry Brigade.

Copy No.	1	Operation Orders File.	
,,	2	War Diary.	
,,	3	47th Division.	By Signal Section.
,,	4	4th Bn. London Regt.	,,
,,	5	6th do.	,,
,,	6	7th do.	,,
,,	7	8th do.	,,
,,	8	15th do.	,,
,,	9	Machine Gun Company	,,
,,	10	Brigade Grenadier Officer	,,
,,	11	47/1 Light Mortar Battery	,,
,,	12	No. 7 Trench Mortar Battery	,,
,,	13	O.C., Bde. Ammn. Reserve	,,
,,	14	141st Infantry Brigade	,,
,,	15	142nd do.	,,
,,	16		

140th INFANTRY BRIGADE

TABLE TO ACCOMPANY OPERATION ORDER NO. 58.

Relieving Unit	Unit to be Relieved	Sub-section	Time for guides to meet units	Meeting place for guides
8th Bn. London Regiment	8th Bn. London Regiment	Right sub-section	7.15 p.m.	MINE GATE, ROSS E. R. BARDO, N.S.A.4.7.
do.	17th	Centre do.	6.15 p.m.	
do.	19th	Left do.	5.15 p.m.	
do.	20th	do.	8.15 p.m.	
140th Bde. Machine Gun Company	141st Bde. Machine Gun Company	Support	4.45 p.m.	
47/1 Light Mortar Battery	47/2 Light Mortar Battery	Right sub-section	To be arranged between Commanding Officers of units concerned.	
140th Bde. Grenadier Coy.	141st Brigade Grenadier Company	In sub-sections held by their respective Battalions.	Grenadier platoons will accompany their Battns.	
140th Bde. Lewis Gun Sections	141st Bde. Lewis Gun Sections	In sub-sections held by their respective Battalions.	9.0 p.m.	

SECRET.

Copy No. 7

140th INFANTRY BRIGADE

OPERATION ORDER No. 56.

14th January, 1916.

1. The following re-adjustments of the line will be made on night 15th/16th January, 1916. After re-adjustment, the limits of LOOS Sector will be from M.5.a.3½.2 to G.36.d.4.2½ (LOOS - ST. LAURENT Road inclusive).

   The 15th Bn. London Regiment will be relieved by the 7th Cameron Highlanders under arrangements to be made by Officers Commanding Units concerned.

   On relief the 15th Bn. London Regiment will be in support disposed as follows:-
   Battalion Headquarters) G.34.c.7.7 and trenches
   and 1 Company) in vicinity
   1 Company in TRANCHEE DE L'UNION between G.35.a.7.4 and G.35.a.5.8
   ~~1 Company 7th Bn. London Regiment in G.36.a.1.0.~~
   2 Companies in NORTH MAROC about M.2.b.1.5.

   All trench stores, except steel helmets, gum boots, Vermorel sprayers, Salvus sets and rifle grenade stands will be handed over on relief.

2. The 7th Bn. London Regiment will occupy the line M.5.a.3½.2 - M.5.b.6.2 (LENS - BETHUNE Road exclusive), now held by the 24th Bn. London Regiment on right and 8th Bn. London Regiment on left.

   Details of reliefs to be arranged by Officers Commanding Units concerned. Relief to commence at 5 p.m.

   7th Battalion Headquarters will be in cellars about G.35.b.4½.1.

   24th Bn. London Regiment is not handing over steel helmets.

3. Alterations in the distribution of the Brigade Machine Gun Company will be notified later.

4. Completion of reliefs will be reported to Brigade Headquarters.

5. After the re-adjustment
   (a) The boundary between 15th and 47th Divisions will be the LOOS - ST. LAURENT Road - Road junction G.36.a.central - thence the present boundary. Use may be made of the communication trench in G.36.a and c. to reach the communication trench in G.36.d leading to front line East of LOOS CRASSIER.
   (b) The boundary between the MAROC and LOOS Sections will be M.5.a.3.2 - VALLEY Cross Roads G.35.c.2.4 - thence along BOYAU DU SUD (which will be common to both Sections for traffic but allotted to MAROC Section for occupation) - MAISON DES MITRAILLEURS - Centre of HARROW Road.

J H Wortley

Captain,
Brigade Major,
140th Infantry Brigade.

Copy No.	1	Operation Orders File.	
,,	2	War Diary.	
,,	3	47th Division.	By Signal Section.
,,	4	4th Bn. London Regt.	,,
,,	5	6th do.	,,
,,	6	7th do.	,,
,,	7	8th do.	,,
,,	8	15th do.	,,
,,	9	Machine Gun Company	,,
,,	10	Brigade Grenadier Officer	,,
,,	11	O.C., Bde. Ammn. Reserve	,,
,,	12	Brigade Transport Officer	,,
,,	13	No. 8 Trench Mortar Bty.	,,
,,	14	142nd Infantry Brigade	,,
,,	15	1/4th Field Company, R.E.	,,

SECRET.

Copy No. 7

140th INFANTRY BRIGADE
OPERATION ORDER No. 57.

19th January, 1916.

Reference – Trench Map, Sheet 36B, 1/40000.

1. The Brigade (less the 4th Bn. London Regiment) will be relieved by the 142nd Infantry Brigade in LOOS Section on the night of 20th/21st January, 1916.

2. The Brigade on relief will be in Divisional Reserve.

3. The 8th Bn. London Regiment will be at the call of the General Officer Commanding MAROC Section, the 15th Bn. London Regiment at the call of General Officer Commanding LOOS Section, as Brigade reserves, if required tactically. They will be at one hour's notice, and Officers Commanding will report to General Officers Commanding the respective Brigades.

4. Reliefs will take place in accordance with attached Table.
Lewis Gun Sections will move in with their Battalions.
The platoons of the 7th Leinster Regiment attached to the 6th and 8th Battalions will move out as with these units, and will rejoin their Battalions at MAROC.
Grenadiers on relief will be billeted with their Battalions.

5. Brigade and Sub-section dumps will be handed over by 4 p.m. 20th January, 1916.

6. No. 2 Trench Mortar Battery will remain in the line.

7. Trench stores, including steel helmets, but excluding gum boots, will be handed over.
Consolidated lists of Trench Stores handed over will be forwarded to Brigade Headquarters by 12 noon on 20th January, 1916.

8. On relief, 47/1 Light Mortar Battery will bring guns out of the line with them.

9. Completion of relief will be reported to Brigade Headquarters, which will remain in its present position.

H.M.Westley

Captain,
Brigade Major,
140th Infantry Brigade.

Copy No.	1	Operation Orders File.	
,,	2	War Diary.	
,,	3	47th Division	By Signal Section.
,,	4	4th Bn. London Regt.	,,
,,	5	6th do.	,,
,,	6	7th do.	,,
,,	7	8th do.	,,
,,	8	15th do.	,,
,,	9	Machine Gun Company	,,
,,	10	Bde. Grenadier Officer	,,
,,	11	Bde. Transport Officer	,,
,,	12	47/1 Light Mortar Bty.	,,
,,	13	No. 8 Trench Mortar Bty.	,,
,,	14	Officer i/c Bde. Amm. Reserve	,,
,,	15	141st Infantry Brigade	,,
,,	16	142nd do.	,,
,,	17	7th Leinster Regt.	,,
,,	18	1/4 Field Company, R.E.	,,

192

140th INFANTRY BRIGADE

TABLE TO ACCOMPANY OPERATION ORDER No. 37.

Relieved Unit	From	To	Relieving Unit	Times for reliefs. 4 per Company, at Iron Gates, NARROW ROAD.	Remarks
Machine Gun Coy.	Trenches	LES BREBIS	142nd Brigade Machine Gun Coy.	1.30 p.m.	Guns in back lines will be relieved in the afternoon. Those in front lines after dusk.
Sharpshooters	Trenches	Rejoin units	142nd Brigade Sharpshooters.	3.45 p.m.	
15th Bn. London Regt.	Left Subsection	LES BREBIS	22nd Bn. London Regt.	4.30 p.m.	
do.	Centre Subsection	do.	21st do.	5.0 p.m.	
do.	Right Subsection	BRACQUEMONT	23rd do.	5.30 p.m.	
do.	Support Trench	NOEUX-LES-MINES	24th do.	6.0 p.m.	
47/1 Light Mortar Battery.	Trenches	LES BREBIS	47/3 Light Mortar Battery.	6.30 p.m.	

SECRET.   Copy No. 7

140th INFANTRY BRIGADE

OPERATION ORDER No. 58.

22nd January 1916.

Reference Map – Secret Blue Print 1/10000.

1. The 140th Infantry Brigade will relieve the 141st Infantry Brigade in the LABOC Section on the night 24th/25th January, 1916.
Movement in accordance with attached table.

2. Four platoons of the 8th Bn. Royal Munster Fusiliers will be attached for instruction, two platoons to the 7th Bn. London Regiment and two platoons to the 15th Bn. London Regiment. These platoons will move in with the Battalions to which they are attached, and will be 48 hours in support lines, when they will be relieved by another four platoons.

3. The Divisional and two Brigade S.A.A. and bomb dumps will be taken over by 4 p.m., 24th January, 1916. The support battalion will furnish a guard of 1 N.C.O. and 3 men over the Divisional dump in HARROW ROAD at point H.2.a.8.9 and the 7th and 15th Bns. London Regiment will furnish 1 N.C.O. and man each as Storemen for the Brigade dumps at H.2.b.1.1 and H.3.a.7.8, respectively. Lists of stores contained in the Divisional and Brigade dumps will be forwarded to Brigade Headquarters by 12 noon on 25th January.

4. Steel helmets will be taken over on relief.

5. Reports to Brigade Headquarters which will remain in present position.

H H Mc.Kay.
Captain,
Brigade Major,
140th Infantry Brigade.

Copy No.	1	Operation Orders File	
	2	War Diary.	
	3	47th Division	By Signal Section.
	4	4th Bn. London Regt.	"
	5	6th Bn. do.	"
	6	7th Bn. do.	"
	7	8th Bn. do.	"
	8	15th Bn. do.	"
	9	Machine Gun Company	"
	10	Brigade Grenadier Officer	"
	11	Brigade Transport Officer	"
	12	Officer i/c Bde. Amm. Reserve	"
	13	47/1 Light Mortar Battery	"
	14	141st Infantry Brigade	"
	15	142nd do.	"
	16	168nd French Brigade	"
	17	8th Bn. Royal Munster Fus.	"
	18	1/3rd Field Company, R.E.	"

140th INFANTRY BRIGADE

TABLE ACCOMPANYING OPERATION ORDER No. 78.

Relieving Unit	Relieved Unit	Destination	Time for Guides at Iron Gates N.2.a.5.0.	Remarks
Brigade Machine Gun Coy.	141st Bde. Machine Gun Coy.	MAROC Section	1.30 p.m.	Will relieve regrouped guns by daylight. Front line guns after dark.
Sharpshooters	141st Bde. Sharpshooters	do.	2.45 p.m.	141st Infy. Bde. Sharp-shooters stay in 24 hours.
6th Bn. London Regiment	16th Bn. London Regiment	"C" or Left Subsection	3.15 p.m.	
15th (with 2 Platoons Royal Munster Fusiliers).	20th	"B" or Centre "	3.45 p.m.	
4th Bn. London Regiment	17th	M.9.b.3.7 - M.9.b.4.4 (Trench C exclusive) Remainder of "A" or Right Subsection.	6.15 p.m.	
7th (with 2 Platoons Royal Munster Fusiliers).	do.			
8th Bn. London Regiment	19th	Support	6.45 p.m.	
47/1 Light Mortar Bty.	47/2 Light Mortar Bty.	MAROC Section	3.30 p.m.	

195

SECRET.

Copy No. 6

140th INFANTRY BRIGADE.

Operation Order No. 59.

(Ref. Blue Print Map, 1/10,000.

31st January 1916.

1. The Brigade will be relieved by 142nd Inf. Bde. in MAROC Section on night February 1st/2nd, and will move into Divisional Reserve. Movements in accordance with attached table.

2. After relief, 7th Battalion Lon. Regt. will be at the call of G.O.C. MAROC Section, and 6th Battalion Lon. Regt. of G.O.C. LOOS Section, and will be at one hour's notice.

3. Platoons of 8th Royal Munster Fusiliers will move out with the Battalions to which they are attached for instruction, and will rejoin their Unit at LES BREBIS.
   Headquarters and two Companies, 8th R.M. Fusiliers will move to LES BREBIS after relief by 9th R.M. Fusiliers.

4. Divisional, Brigade and Subsection Dumps, and control posts will be handed over by 4 p.m. on February 1st.
   N.C.O i/c road gangs, 142nd Infantry Brigade will report at 7th Battalion Headquarters at Noon on February 1st.

5. Trench Stores will be handed over and receipts taken, special receipts being obtained for steel helmets. Copies of receipts given will be forwarded to Brigade Headquarters by noon February 2nd.

6. Reports to Brigade Headquarters, which will remain in present position.

for Captain.
Brigade Major,
140th Infantry Brigade.

```
Copy No. 1   Operation Order File.
  ,,     2   War Diary.
  ,,     3   4th Bn. Lon. Regt.          By Signal Service.
  ,,     4   6th     do.                 do.
  ,,     5   7th     do.                 do.
  ,,     6   8th     do.                 do.
  ,,     7   15th    do.                 do.
  ,,     8   47th Division.              do.
  ,,     9   8th Royal Munster Fus.      do.
  ,,    10   A/140 Light Mortar Battery. do.
  ,,    11   7th Trench Mortar Battery.  do.
  ,,    12   Brigade Grenadier Offr.     do.
  ,,    13   Brigade Transport Offr.     do.
  ,,    14   Brigade Amm. Reserve Offr.  do.
  ,,    15   141st Inf. Brigade.         do.
  ,,    16.  142nd Inf. Brigade.         do.
  ,,    17   162nd French Brigade.       do.
```

RELIEF TABLE issued with Operation Order no. 59.

Unit.	Relieving Unit.	Section.	Billets on relief.	Billets at Iron Gates, S.MAROC.	p.m.	Remarks.
Sharpshooters	142nd Sharpshooters.			With Units.	5. 0	Will remain in 24 hours after relief.
15th Battn.	22nd Battn.	Centre.	Braquemont.		5.30	
8th Battn.)	21st Battn.	Right.	Braquemont.)			
4th Battn.)			Haillicourt.)		6. 0	
6th Battn.	24th Battn.	Left.	Les Brebis &* Nth Maroc.		6.30	* 2 Companies, 2 Lewis Guns and 2 Sections Grenadiers of 6th and 7th Battalions will occupy the billets in North and South Maroc vacated respectively by 24th and 23rd Battalions.
7th Battn.	23rd Battn.	Support.	Les Brebis & * Sth Maroc.		7. 0	
Bde. M.G.Coy.	142nd Bde M.G.Coy.	Trenches	Les Brebis.		10. 0	
A/140 L.M.B.	A/142nd L.M.B.	"	Les Brebis.		10.10	

197

Army Form C. 2118

WAR DIARY
or
~~INTELLIGENCE~~ SUMMARY
(Erase heading not required.)

8th London Regt.
Post Office Rifles
February 1916.

Place	Date	Hour	Summary of Events and Information	Remarks and references to Appendices
Souchez Mines Noeux-les-Mines (Bruquemont)	1	-	The 140th Bde coming into Divl. Reserve, the Bn. was relieved by the 21st London Rifs. & moved to Noeux-les-Mines (Bruquemont) - Relief commenced 6 p.m.	
Noeux-les-Mines (Bruquemont)	2-4	-	Bn. remained in billets at Noeux-les-Mines (Bruquemont)	
Loos	5	-	Bn. left Noeux-les-Mines (Bruquemont) at 3.30, marched via Les Brebis (where it had teas) to Loos, and took over Right Sub-Section of Loos Sector of trenches from 20th Bn. London Regt.	
"	6-13	-	Bn. remained in the trenches. On 12th a Draft of 20 O.R. joined the Bn. from the 3rd Bn.	
Loos Les Brebis	14	-	In running wire exploded opposite enemy edge Sub. Section. Bn. Lewis gun Detachment cooperated successfully in keeping hole away. Bn. relieved in evening by 1st Gloucester Regt. & marched to billets at Les Brebis for the night. Two O.R. wounded. 47th Divn. relieved by 1st Div., got into Corps Reserve.	
Les Brebis Lillers	15	-	Bn. left Les Brebis at 10 a.m. and marched to Noeux-les-Mines where it entrained for Lillers. Bn. arrived Lillers about 4.30 p.m. & went into billets.	
Lillers	16-28	-	Bn. remained in billets at Lillers. On 20th G.O.C. 1st Army (Sir C. Monro) inspected Bn. & conferred Decorations. On 24th 5 Officers & 17 O.R. joined Bn. from 3rd Bn. On 25th 2/69 A/Cpl Mattock rec'd D.C.M. On 28th 67 O.R. joined from 3rd Bn.	
Lillers	29	-	... Enemy in 1st Army Tday 7 Arras & sent into billets ...	

SECRET.   Copy No. 7

140th INFANTRY BRIGADE
OPERATION ORDER No. 80.

4th February, 1916.

Reference - Blue Print "B".

1. The 140th Infantry Brigade will relieve the 141st Infantry Brigade in LOOS Section tomorrow night, 5th/6th February, 1916.

2. Reliefs will be carried out in accordance with attached schedule.

3. No. 8 Trench Mortar Battery will remain in the line and the Officer Commanding will be quartered with Headquarters of the Battalion in the Centre Sub-section.

4. Receipts will be given for Trench Stores, and copies sent to the Brigade Office by 12 midday, 6th February, 1916.

5. The 4th Bn. London Regiment will remain at MAILLICOURT.

6. Instructions about lorries will be issued when received.

7. Completion of reliefs will be reported to Brigade Headquarters by Priority wire.

                                              Captain,
                                     Acting Brigade Major,
                                     140th Infantry Brigade.

Copy No.		
1	Operation Orders File.	
2	War Diary.	
3	47th Division	By Signal Section.
4	4th Bn. London Regiment	"
5	6th do.	"
6	7th do.	"
7	8th do.	"
8	15th do.	"
9	Machine Gun Company	"
10	A/140 Light Mortar Battery	"
11	No. 8 Trench Mortar Battery	"
12	Brigade Grenadier Officer	"
13	Brigade Transport Officer	"
14	Officer i/c Bde. Ammn. Reserve	"
15	141st Infantry Brigade	"
16	142nd do.	"
17	9th Bn. Royal Dublin Fusiliers	"
18	1/3rd Field Company, R.E.	"

140th INFANTRY BRIGADE

SCHEME TO ACCOMPANY OPERATION ORDER NO. 20.

Unit	Sub-section	Units of 141st Infantry Brigade	Guides at gates of TOWER, MORTAR RANGE.	Remarks
6th Bn. London Regiment	Left	16th Bn. London Regiment	6.30 p.m.	
7th do.	Centre	17th do.	6. 0 p.m.	
8th do.	Right	20th do.	6.30 p.m.	
15th do.	Support	19th do.	7. 0 p.m.	
Machine Gun Company		Machine Gun Company	10. 0 p.m.	
A/140 Light Mortar Battery		A/141 Light Mortar Battery	5. 0 p.m.	
Sharpshooters		Sharpshooters	3. 0 p.m.	

NOTE:- Lewis guns will move in with their battalions.

202

SECRET.   Copy No. 6

140th INFANTRY BRIGADE

OPERATION ORDER No. 61.

Reference - New Secret blue print.   8th February, 1916.

1. The 15th Bn. London Regiment will relieve the 6th Bn. London Regiment in LOOS Left Sub-section tomorrow evening 9th/10th February, 1916.

2. Arrangements will be made direct between Battalions concerned.

3. 15th Bn. London Regiment will pass 6th Bn. London Regiment Headquarters at 6.30 p.m.

4. 1 Company of the 9th Royal Dublin Fusiliers will move into LOOS Right Sub-section tomorrow evening, 9th/10th February, 1916. They will come under orders of the Officer Commanding 8th Bn. London Regiment, who will place them in the front line, withdrawing into support one of his own Companies.

5. Guides for the Royal Dublin Fusiliers (1 per Platoon) will meet them at the gates of FOSSE No. 5, NORTH MAROC, at 6.30 p.m.

6. 7.45 p.m. Completion of reliefs will be reported to Brigade Headquarters by Priority wire.

R V Foster Captain,
Brigade Major,
140th Infantry Brigade.

Copy No. 1	Operation Orders File.	
,, 2	War Diary.	
,, 3	47th Division	By Signal Section.
,, 4	6th London Regt.	,,
,, 5	7th do.	,,
,, 6	8th do.	,,
,, 7	15th do.	,,
,, 8	Machine Gun Company	,,
,, 9	Brigade Grenadier Officer.	,,
,, 10	Brigade Transport Officer	,,
,, 11	Bde. Ammn. Reserve Officer	,,
,, 12	9th Royal Dublin Fusiliers	,,
,, 13	141st Infy. Brigade	,,
,, 14	142nd do.	,,
,, 15	45th do.	,,
,, 16	2/3rd Field Company, R.E.	,,

SECRET.

140th Infantry Brigade.

1. A Wireless Telegraph Station has been established at the Headquarters of the Commandant LOOS and is in communication with Div. Hdqrs. via. MAZINGARBE.

2. This means of communication is to be used only for URGENT tactical messages and then only when all other telegraphic means of communication have failed.

3. Messages will be sent in clear, and can be sent to either Div. Hdqrs. Div. Arty. or G.O.C. Bde. holding LOOS Section.

4. The detachment, 3 men, will be attached for administration to the battalion occupying LOOS Defences and will be relieved as required by O.C. Wireless 1st Army.

G/701/45.
10th Feb. 1916.

(sd) B. BURNETT HITCHCOCK,
Lt. Colonel,
General Staff,
47th (London) Division.

Officer Commanding,
8th Bn. London Regiment.

For your information, please.

Captain,
Brigade Major,
140th Infantry Brigade.

SECRET.

Officer Commanding,

8th Bn. London Regiment.

Billets are allotted to Battalions as shown in the attached map, with the following exceptions:-

6th Battalion Area.
4th London Field Ambulance will occupy No. 2, PLACE DE L'EGLISE and the FERME DE COMPIEGNE, also the house next door to it which will be their Officers' Mess.

7th Battalion Area.
The Marché Convent is not to be used.
The Brigade Grenadiers will occupy billets in RUE DU PROMENADE, but their Officers will be in GRANDE PLACE.

8th Battalion Area.
A portion of the 47th Divisional Salvage Company, 1 Officer and a small number of men, will be billeted in this area.

Billeting parties will proceed by train to LILLERS on 14th February, 1916, leaving NOEUX-LES-MINES Station at 11 a.m. and will report to the Staff Captain, 2nd Infantry Brigade, at Brigade Headquarters, who will send guides with them to the various Quartermasters' Stores.

Should any difficulties arise, application should be made to the Town Major in RUE NATIONALE.

Interpreters will be allotted as under:-
Interpreter de CAUX, 8th Bn. London Regiment, will be at the disposal of the 6th Bn. London Regiment, until 3 p.m. on the 14th instant; after which he will be attached to the 7th Bn. London Regiment.

Interpreter DIEBOLT, 6th Bn. London Regiment, will be at the disposal of the 8th Bn. London Regiment, until 3 p.m. on the 14th instant; after which he will be attached to the 15th Bn. London Regiment.

The Brigade Machine Gun Company will be billeted in HAUT RIEUX. They will take over billets now occupied by "C" Squadron Northumberland Hussars. One Officer or N.C.O. should be sent as advance billeting party.

Major,
Staff Captain,
140th Infantry Brigade.

BRIGADE OFFICE
1 1 FEB. 1916

N.B.   All billeting parties must carry one day's rations.
Orders for billets for A/140 Light Mortar Battery will be issued by wire later.

205

SECRET.   Copy No. 6

140th INFANTRY BRIGADE.

OPERATION ORDER No. 62.

Reference map -   1/40000 Sheets 36A, 36B & 36C.

                                                   12th February, 1916.

1. The 140th Infantry Brigade will be relieved by the 3rd Infantry Brigade in the LOOS Sector on the night of 14th/15th February, 1916.
   On the 15th February, 1916, the 140th Infantry Brigade will be relieved by the 2nd Infantry Brigade in Divisional Reserve. The Brigade will then move into Army Reserve at LILLERS.

2. Reliefs will be carried out in accordance with attached Table Appendix 1.

3. The Section is rearranged by the 3rd Infantry Brigade as follows:-
   Right Sub-section - Headquarters: Present Centre Sub-section Headquarters.
                        2 Companies in front line.
                        1 Company in SOUTH STREET.
                        1 Company in cellars near Battalion Headquarters.
   Left Sub-section. - Headquarters: Present Left Sub-section Headquarters.
                        2 Companies in Front Line.
                        1 Company in REGENT STREET.
                        1 Company in ENCLOSURE.
   The division between the Sub-sections is where the Front Line joins the "D" at M.6.c.0.7.

4. Lewis guns will move in with Battalions, one guide per Lewis gun being sent. Guides will be told which Sub-section Battalion they are for.

5. The Officer Commanding 15th Bn. London Regiment will send an N.C.O. to organise guides at FOSSE 5 for Left Sub-section Battalion.
   The Officer Commanding 8th Bn. London Regiment will send an N.C.O. to organise guides for Right Sub-section Battalion.

6. Battalions will each send a guide to the hole in the wall, NORTH MAROC, at 12-30 p.m. to conduct N.C.O's to Battalion Headquarters to take over stores.

7. All trench stores, except steel helmets and rifle grenade guns, will be handed over on relief. Copies of receipts to be at Brigade Headquarters by 6 p.m., 15th February, 1916.

8. Officer Commanding A/140 Light Mortar Battery, will hand over 3 guns to the 3rd Infantry Brigade.

9. The section of the Machine Gun Company attached to the 4th Bn. Royal Welch Fusiliers as part of the garrison of LOOS will remain under the orders of the 4th Bn. Royal Welch Fusiliers until arrival in the new area, when they will rejoin their own Brigade on the afternoon of 16th February, 1916.

10. Sharpshooters will come out of the line with their Battalions.

11.	Completion of relief to be reported to Brigade Headquarters by Priority wire.

12.	Battalions will detach their parties for the 173rd Tunnelling Company on arrival at NOEUX-les-MINES, on 15th February, 1916.

13.	March table for transport is in Appendix 11.

14.	Brigade Headquarters will close at 9 a.m. on the 15th February, 1916, and will re-open at the MAJOR'S HOUSE, LILLERS, on arrival.

[signature]
Major

for Brigade Major,
140th Infantry Brigade.

```
Copy No.  1    Operation Orders File.
    ,,    2    War Diary.
    ,,    3    47th Division            By Signal Section.
    ,,    4    6th Bn. London Regt.           ,,
    ,,    5    7th      do                    ,,
    ,,    6    8th      do                    ,,
    ,,    7    15th     do                    ,,
    ,,    8    Machine Gun Company            ,,
    ,,    9    Brigade Sharpshooters          ,,
    ,,   10    Bde. Ammn. Reserve Officer     ,,
    ,,   11    Bde. Grenadier Officer         ,,
    ,,   12    Bde. Transport Officer         ,,
    ,,   13    A/140 Light Mortar Battery     ,,
    ,,   14    No. 8 Trench Mortar Battery    ,,
    ,,   15    3rd Infantry Brigade           ,,
    ,,   16    2nd      do.                   ,,
    ,,   17    141st    do.                   ,,
    ,,   18    45th     do.                   ,,
```

140th INFANTRY BRIGADE.

APPENDIX I.

Unit	Sub-section	Relieving unit	Guides at Mine gates of FOSSE 5, NORTH MAROC.	Billets for night 14th/15th February.	Time at which Bns.will arrive at NOEUX-LES-MINES Station 15th February.		Remarks
4th Bn.Lond.Regt.	Support	1st Bn.Sth.Wales Bord.	6.30 p.m.	BRAQUEMONT	9.35 a.m.		(1) Right Coy. Right of New Subsection to CHALK PIT (exclusive). (2) Support - REGENT ST. (3) Reserve - ENCLOSURE Battalion Headquarters.
7th do.	Left Right	2nd Bn.Munster Fus. 1st Bn. Gloucesters	5.30 p.m. 6. 0 p.m.	}BRAQUEMONT	11.55 12.5 p.m.	3 Guides (Left) 1 Guide (Right)	
8th do.	Right	1st Bn. Gloucesters	6. 0 p.m.	LES BREBIS	½ Bn. 11.55 am ½ Bn.12.5 Bn.2.35 p.m.	4 Guides	(1) Right Coy. Right of Section to M.5.d.3.9. (2) Left Coy.M.5.d.3.9 left of Subsection. (3) Support Coy. (4) Reserve Coy.
15th do.	Left	2nd Bn.Munster Fus.	5.30 p.m.	LES BREBIS	2.35 p.m.	2 Guides	(1) Headquarters. (2) Left Coy.from CHALK PIT exclusive - left of Section.
Machine Gun Coy.	---	Machine Gun Coy.	10.0 p.m.	LES BREBIS	11.55 am 12.5 p.m.		
A/140 L.M.B.	---	1/3rd L.M.B.	7.0 p.m.	LES BREBIS	2.35 p.m.		

140th INFANTRY BRIGADE

APPENDIX II.

The First Line Transport (with Baggage Wagons) will move to LILLERS on the morning of the 15th February, via the Cross Roads L.22.d., HALTE L.27.d and the ARRAS road to NOEUX-LES-MINES, over the level crossing at E.17.d, then past BETHUNE Railway Station and via ANNEZIN - CHOCQUES, to billets as shown in instructions from the Brigade issued under No. S.C. 521, dated 11th February, 1916.

The heads of Transport of Units will pass the starting point, Road Junction L.29.a., in order as under, and at the times stated in Table. Intervals of 50 yards will be kept between each pair of vehicles:-

1. 15th Bn. London Regiment — 6. 0 a.m.
2. 6th   do.   — 6.20 a.m.
3. 8th   do.   — 6.40 a.m.
4. Brigade Headquarters   — 7. 0 a.m.
5. 7th Bn. London Regiment — 7.10 a.m.
6. Half of Brigade Machine Gun Coy. — 7.30 a.m.

The head of the column will halt at Road Junction L.19.a in ARRAS Road, and the wagons of all units will close up leaving an interval of 30 yards between each Unit.

The Transport Officer of the 6th Battalion will ride in rear of the column, and will see that there is no straggling, etc.

Two draught horses, harnessed with lead sets, will be detailed (one by the 7th Battalion and one by the 6th Battalion) to march in rear of the column for use in case of emergency, at the discretion of the Transport Officer of the 6th Battalion.

Transport Officers will ride with their units and will be responsible for the march discipline.

Feeds will be taken for all horses and water buckets will be carried where they are easily accessible.

Water carts should be filled and used for watering horses at the midday halt.

SECRET.

109.

OFFICER COMMANDING,
    8th Bn. London Regiment.

1. From midnight Feb 17th/18th to midnight Feb.24th/25th. 47th Division will be in G.H.Q. Reserve and will be held in readiness to entrain at 9 hours notice in accordance with scheme to be issued later.

2. During this period the instructions re Battalions being at 3 hours notice will be cancelled.

3. Acknowledge.

C/535
16/2/16.

                      Captain,
                  Brigade Major,
            140th Infantry Brigade.

SECRET

140th INFANTRY BRIGADE.

Copy No. 6

Operation Order No. 83-

Reference.

Belgium-Hazebrouck.5a. 1/100,000.   28.2.16.

1.   The 140th Infantry Brigade with detachment of 4th London Field Ambulance and No. 2 Coy. Divisional Train will move to 1st Army training area tomorrow, the 29th instant, via ST.HILAIRE-RELY-LA TIRMOND-CUHEM and take over billets at present occupied by 142nd Brigade and attached troops.

2.   The move will be carried out in accordance with attached March table.

3.   1st Line Transport will be brigaded under the orders of Brigade Transport Officer in order of march of units.
     Each unit will detail one half Company to march behind their own 1st line transport. They will be prepared to assist the transport if in difficulties.
     1st line transport will leave the transport column at the same places as detailed in the march table for their own units.
     1st line transport will be packed in accordance with load tables.

4.   Separate instructions have been issued for motor lorries.

5.   Baggage wagons will move with 1st line transport of their own units.

6.   Refilling point is at BASSE BOULOGNE. Cyclist guides will be sent from each unit to be there at 2 p.m.

7.   The halt at 8.50 a.m. will NOT be observed.

8.   Brigade Headquarters will close at LILLERS at 8.30 a.m. and will reopen on arrival at ERNY-ST-JULIEN.

Issued at

                                        Lieut.
                                   for Brigade Major,
                                  140th Infantry Brigade.

Copy No.1. War Diary.
       2. File.
       3. 47th Division.   (By Signal Section)
       4. 6th Battn.   do.
       5. 7th   ,,   do.
       6. 8th   ,,   do.
       7. 15th   ,,   do.
       8. Machine Gun Coy.   do.
       9. Transport Officer.   do.
      10. 4th Field Ambulance.   do.
      11. No.2 Coy.47th Div.Train.   do.
      12. 142nd Inf. Bde.   do.
      13. Spare.   do.
      14.   ,,   do.

SECRET.

PROGRAMME OF MOVE OF 47th DIVISION FROM 1st ARMY.

No. of Train.	Type of Train.	Entrain at.	Time of Departure.	Serial No.	UNIT.	Detrain at.	Arrive (approx).
1	C	LILLERS	0.00	01 05 02 85	Divisional H.Q. Div. Sig. Co. H.Q. & No.1 Section. H.Q. Div. Artillery. H.Q. Div. Engineers.		
2	C	FOUQUEREUIL.	1.00	30 35 92 36	H.Q. 142nd Inf. Bde. No.4 Sec. Sig. Co. No.4 Co. Div. Train. H.Q. 142nd Bde Machine Gun Co.		
3	C	BERGUETTE.	2.00	10 15 90 40 16	H.Q. 140th Inf. Bde. No.2 Sec. Sig. Co. No.2 Co. Div. Train. H.Q. 1/5th London Bde R.F.A. H.Q. 140th Bde Machine Gun Co.		
4	C	LILLERS.	3.00	20 25 91 50 26	H.Q. 141st Inf. Bde. No.3 Sec. Sig. Co. No.3 Co. Div. Train. H.Q. 1/6th London Bde R.F.A. H.Q. 141st Bde Machine Gun Co.		
5	C	FOUQUEREUIL.	4.00	31 36	1/21st London Regt. 1 Section 142nd Bde Machine Gun Co.		
6	C	BERGUETTE.	5.00	11 16	1/6th London Regt. 1 Section 140th Bde Machine Gun Co.		
7	C	LILLERS.	6.00	21 26	1/17th London Regt. 1 Section 141st Bde Machine Gun Co.		
8	C	FOUQUEREUIL.	7.00	32 36	1/22nd London Regt. 1 Section 142nd Bde Machine Gun Co.		

-2-

No. of Train.	Type of Train.	Entrain at.	Time of Departure.	Serial No.	UNIT.	Detrain at.	Arrive (approx.).
9	C	BERGUETTE.	8.00	12 16	1/7th London Regt. 1 Section 140th Bde Machine Gun Co.		
10	C	LILLERS.	9.00	22 26	1/18th London Regt. 1 Section 141st Bde Machine Gun Co.		
11	C	FOUQUEREUIL.	10.00	33 36	1/23rd London Regt. 1 Section 142nd Bde Machine Gun Co.		
12	C	BERGUETTE.	11.00	13 16	1/8th London Regt. 1 Section 140th Bde Machine Gun Co.		
13	C	LILLERS.	12.00	23 26	1/19th London Regt. 1 Section 141st Bde Machine Gun Co.		
14	C	FOUQUEREUIL.	13.00	34 36	1/24th London Regt. 1 Section 142nd Bde Machine Gun Co.		
15	C	BERGUETTE.	14.00	14 16	1/15th London Regt. 1 Section 140th Bde Machine Gun Co.		
16	C	LILLERS.	15.00	24 26	1/20th London Regt. 1 Section 141st Bde Machine Gun Co.		
17	C	FOUQUEREUIL.	16.00	87 08	1/4th London Field Co. R.E. 8th Trench Mortar Battery.		
18	C	BERGUETTE.	17.00	41 45	12th London Battery R.F.A. 1/3rd Ammn. Col. 1/5th London Bde R.F.A.		
19	C	LILLERS.	18.00	51 55	15th London Battery R.F.A. 1/3rd Ammn. Col. 1/6th London Bde R.F.A.		
20	C	FOUQUEREUIL.	19.00	86 07	1/3rd London Field Co. R.E. 7th Trench Mortar Battery.		

254

No. of Train.	Type of Train.	Entrain at.	Time of Departure.	Serial No.	UNIT.	Detrain at.	Arrive (Approx.)
21	C	BERGUETTE.	20.00	43 45	14th London Battery R.F.A. 1/3rd Ammn. Col. 1/5th London Bde R.F.A.		
22	C	LILLERS.	21.00	53 55	17th London Battery R.F.A. 1/3rd Ammn. Col. 1/6th London Bde R.F.A.		
23	C	FOUQUEREUIL.	22.00	88	2/3rd London Field Co. R.E.		
24	C	BERGUETTE.	23.00	42 45	13th London Battery R.F.A. 1/3rd Ammn. Col. 1/5th London Bde R.F.A.		
25	C	LILLERS.	24.00	52 55	16th London Battery R.F.A. 1/3rd Ammn. Col. 1/6th London Bde R.F.A.		
26	C	FOUQUEREUIL.	1.00	70 71 75	H.Q. 1/8th London Bde Howitzer. 21st London Battery R.F.A. How: 1/3rd Ammn. Col. 1/8th London Bde R.F.A. How.		
27	C	BERGUETTE.	2.00	93 60 96	1/4th London Field Ambulance. H.Q. 1/7th London Bde R.F.A. 47th Div. Sanitary Section.		
28	C	LILLERS.	3.00	95 98	1/6th London Field Ambulance. Salvage Co.		
29	C	FOUQUEREUIL.	4.00	73 75	B.176 Howitzer Battery. 1/3rd Ammn. Col. 1/8th London Bde R.F.A. How.		
30	C	BERGUETTE.	5.00	61 65	18th London Battery R.F.A. 1/3rd Ammn. Col. 1/7th London Bde R.F.A.		
31	C	LILLERS.	6.00	03 06	"C" Squad. 1/1st King Edward's Horse. Div. Cyclist Co.		
32	C	FOUQUEREUIL.	7.00	72 75	22nd London Battery R.F.A. How. 1/3rd Ammn. Col. 1/8th London Bde R.F.A. How.		

-4-

No. of Train.	Type of Train.	Entrain at.	Time of Departure.	Serial No.	UNIT.	Detrain at.	Arrive (Approx.)
33	C	BERGUETTE.	8.00	63 65	20th London Battery R.F.A. 1/3rd Ammn. Col. 1/7th London Bde R.F.A.		
34	C	LILLERS.	9.00	94 97	1/5th London Field Ambulance. 1/2nd London Mobile Veterinary Section.		
35	P	FOUQUEREUIL.	10.00	04	Pioneer Bn. 1/4th R.W. Fus. (Personnel not to exceed 500).		
36	C	BERGUETTE.	11.00	62 65	19th London Battery R.F.A. 1/3rd Ammn. Col. 1/7th London Bde R.F.A.		
37	P	LILLERS.	12.00	89 80 84	H.Q. & H.Q. Co. Div. Train. H.Q. Div. Ammn. Column. No.4 Section Div. Ammn. Column.		
38	P	FOUQUEREUIL.	13.00	83 04	No.3 Sec'n Div. Ammn. Column. 4th R.W.F. (remaining personnel).		
39	P	BERGUETTE.	14.00	82	No.2 Sec'n Div. Ammn. Column.		
40	P	LILLERS.	15.00	81	No.1 Sec'n Div. Ammn. Column.		

BETHUNE.
12-2-16.

Sjd H.C.J.HILDYARD,
Lieut. Colonel,
A.D.R.T., Southern Railheads.

S E C R E T.

TABLE "D" - 47th DIVISION.

Unit.	Serial No.	DESCRIPTION.
Divisional Units.	4701	Divisional Headquarters.
	4702	H.Q., Divisional Artillery.
	4703	"C" Squadron 1/1st King Edward's Horse.
	4704	Pioneer Batt., 1/4th R.W.Fus. (T).
	4705	Div. Sig. Co. H.Q., and No.1 Section.
	4706	Div. Cyclist Co.
	4707	7th Trench Mortar Battery.
	4708	8th " " "
140th Infantry Bde.	4710	Brigade H.Q.
	4711	1/6th Batt. London Regt.
	4712	1/7th " " "
	4713	1/8th " " "
	4714	1/15th " " "
	4715	No.2 Section Sig. Co.
	4716	Bde Machine Gun Co.
141st Infantry Bde.	4720	Brigade H.Q.
	4721	1/17th London Regt.
	4722	1/18th " "
	4723	1/19th " "
	4724	1/20th " "
	4725	No.3 Section Sig. Co.
	4726	Bde Machine Gun Co.
142nd Infantry Bde.	4730	Brigade H.Q.
	4731	1/21st London Regt.
	4732	1/22nd " "
	4733	1/23rd " "
	4734	1/24th " "
	4735	No.4 Section Sig. Co.
	4736	Bde Machine Gun Co.
1/5th London Bde., R.F.A.	4740	Brigade H.Q.
	4741	12th London Batt. R.F.A. 4 - 18 pdrs.
	4742	13th " " " " " "
	4743	14th " " " " " "
	4744	
	4745	Bde Ammn. Column.
1/6th London Bde., R.F.A.	4750	Brigade H.Q.
	4751	15th London Batt. R.F.A. 4 - 18 pdrs.
	4752	16th " " " " " "
	4753	17th " " " " " "
	4754	
	4755	Brigade Ammn. Column.
1/7th London Bde., R.F.A.	4760	Brigade H.Q.
	4761	18th London Batt. R.F.A. 4 - 18 pdrs.
	4762	19th " " " " " "
	4763	20th " " " " " "
	4764	
	4765	Brigade Ammn. Column.
1/8th London Bde., R.F.A. (Howitzer).	4770	Brigade H.Q.
	4771	21st London Batt. R.F.A. 4 - 4.5" Hows.
	4772	22nd " " " " " "
	4773	B.176 Howitzer Battery.
	4774	
	4775	Bde Ammn. Column.

Unit.	Serial No.	DESCRIPTION.
47th Div. Ammn. Col.	4780	H.Q.
	4781	No.1 Section.
	4782	No.2 "
	4783	No.3 "
	4784	No.4
47th Div. Engineers.	4785	H.Q.
	4786	1/3rd London Field Co. R.E.
	4787	1/4th " " " "
	4788	2/3rd
47th Div. Train. (less Transport with Troops).	4789	H.Q. & H.Q. Co.
	4790	No.2 Company.
	4791	No.3 "
	4792	No.4
Medical Units.	4793	1/4th London Field Ambulance.
	4794	1/5th " " "
	4795	1/6th
	4796	47th Sanitary Section.
Veterinary Unit.	4797	1/2nd London Mobile Veterinary Section.
	4798	Salvage Company.

Sgd H.C.J.HILDYARD,
Lieut. Colonel,

A.D.R.T., Southern Railheads.

BETHUNE,
12-2-16.

SECRET.

Copy No. 25

1. With reference to 47th Division No. G/701/5/21 dated 14-2-16, herewith Railway Time Table in case of move; also table of routes to be used by troops.

The composition of trains is as follows:-

    Type Combatant.   34 Covered trucks.
                             13 Open flats.
                             1 Officers' Coach.

    Type Parc.   24 Covered trucks.
                             23 Open flats.
                             1 Officers' Coach.

Covered trucks take 40 men or 8 horses; two or three men can travel in each truck with the horses.

Open flats vary in size, but 4 pairs of wheels can be taken with limbered vehicles (5 for guns and ammunition wagons); 3 pairs when 1 4-wheeled vehicle is not limbered, and only 1 vehicle in the case of pontoons and ambulances.

Officers' Coach cannot be taken as having more than 4 compartments.

Troops should be at the Station 3 hours before time of departure of their trains, except in the case of Infantry, whose transport and horses, with a loading party of one officer, 6 N.C.Os. and 50 men, should be at the Station 3 hours before time of departure, the rest of the battalion arriving one hour before.
In all cases an officer will report to the R.T.O. a quarter of an hour before the troops arrive at the Station.

2. Times of departure are not actual times, but are calculated on the zero basis.

Actual detraining stations cannot be shown, as they will be on either of the following lines:-

    CANAPLES - DOULLENS - MENDICOURT PAS.

    AMIENS - MERICOURT.

    AMIENS - GUILLACOURT.

If the move is in the Northern portion of the III Army Area, the route will be FOUQUEREUIL - ST. POL - DOULLENS, and the time taken will be about six hours to DOULLENS.

If the move is to the Southern portion of the III Army Area, the route will be HAZEBROUCK - CALAIS - ABBEVILLE - AMIENS, and the time taken will be 10 hours to AMIENS.

3. The first troops to entrain should be prepared to be at the Station 6 hours after the order for the entrainment is given.

4. Baggage, supply and extra forage wagons will accompany units.
Immediately the warning to move is received, O.J. Divisional Train will send baggage, supply and extra forage wagons to the Headquarters of the Units to which they are attached.

5. Breast ropes for horses must be provided by units in the proportion of 1 breast rope or 2 head ropes per 8 horses.

6. Water carts will be entrained full. Water bottles will be full. Drag ropes will be carried so as to be easily accessible.

7. All Motor Vehicles will proceed by road under orders to be issued later.

8. G.O.C. R.A. will be responsible that sufficient men are detailed to assist in entraining the D.A.C.

Acknowledge

Hdqrtrs,
47th Divn.
S/107.
15-2-16.

[signature]
Lieut. Colonel,
A.A. & Q.M.G., 47th (London) Division.

Copy No:-

1	to	General Staff.
2 to 5	"	"Q" Office.
6	"	4th Corps.
7	"	Camp Commandant.
8	"	"C" Sqdrn, King Edward's Horse.
9	"	Divisional Cyclist Co.
10 to 15	"	" Artillery.
16 " 19	"	" Engineers.
20	"	" Signal Co.
21 " 26	"	140th Infantry Brigade.
27 " 32	"	141st " "
33 " 38	"	142nd " "
39	"	4th Batt. Royal Welsh Fusiliers.
40	"	No. 7 Trench Mortar Battery.
41	"	" 8 " " "
42	"	Divisional Salvage Co.
43 " 47	"	" Train.
48	"	Senior Supply Officer.
49 " 54	"	A.D.M.S.
55 & 56	"	A.D.V.S.
57	"	A.P.M.
58	"	1st Division.

SECRET.   47th (LONDON) DIVISION.

With reference to 47th Division No.S/107, dated 15-2-16:

1. The following lorries for the carriage of blankets will be ordered to report at the various Headquarters as soon as possible after the orders to entrain are received:

   2 Lorries per Battalion to report at Infantry Bde Headquarters

   2   "   for Divisional Engineers, to report at R.E.   "
            LAPUGNOY.

   1 Lorry for Divisional Squadron and Cyclist Co., to report at Headquarters "C" Squadron, K.E.H., HURIONVILLE.

   1   "   for 4th Batt. R. Welsh Fusiliers, to report at Headquarters of that Battn. at MARLES-les-MINES.

   3 Lorries to the Divisional School of Instruction, LABEUVRIERE, for blankets, 2 Trench Mortar Batteries, and Machine Guns.

2. The Instructional Staff and Officers and Men at the Divisional School of Instruction, LABEUVRIERE, and the personnel of the two Trench Mortar Batteries, will march to rejoin their units immediately the lorries are loaded, moving in Brigade parties by the shortest route to their respective Brigade Headquarters, except those whose units are entraining at FOUQUEREUIL, who will move straight to that Station.

3. The Staff, Officers and Men at the Infantry Training School, VAUDRICOURT, will not move and will be rationed under arrangements to be made by 4th Corps.

4. Men employed in the Divisional Laundry, Shoemakers & Tailors Shops, will rejoin their units, but 1 N.C.O. and 2 men of the Laundry Staff will remain in charge of clothing and the disinfecting plant.

5. Men attached to the 173rd Tunnelling Co. will rejoin their units, lorries being sent to bring them from NOEUX-les-MINES.

6. Temporarily Unfit men will all rejoin their units.

7. The A.P.M. will order all men on road control duties to rejoin their units.

8. All surplus kits and baggage will be collected under Brigade arrangements, but not more than 3 men per Battalion are to be left in charge. Companies R.E., Batteries R.F.A., the D.A.C., Divisional Mounted Troops, Divisional Train and Field Ambulances will leave one man each. These men should be chosen from "Temporarily Unfits".

9. The Divisional Salvage Co. will not move with the remainder of the troops, and Capt. FEARON will make the necessary arrangements for the collection and storage of all baggage and property left behind. When this duty has been completed the Salvage Co. will rejoin the Division.

10. The 4th Corps has been asked to make arrangements for rationing the parties left behind, as well as the school at VAUDRICOURT.

Hdqrtrs,
47th Divn.
S/107/1.
15-2-16.

H. J. Nicholl
Captain,
D.A.A. & Q.M.G., 47th (London) Division.

251

SECRET.

MAP Ref:
36ᴬ 1/40000
36ᴮ 1/40000

47th (LONDON) DIVISION.

ROUTE for movement of TROOPS ENTRAINING AT BERGUETTE.

Troops from LILLERS.	via MANQUEVILLE - HAMEN - ARTOIS - Cross roads C.21.c.1.8.
No.2 Co. Div. Train.	via BURBURE to LILLERS, thence as above.
140th Bde M. G. Co.	To LILLERS, thence as above.
Troops from AUCHEL & MARLES-les-MINES.	via LOZINGHEM - HAUT RIEUX - LILLERS, thence as above.

ROUTE for movement of TROOPS ENTRAINING AT LILLERS.

141st Brigade, and Bde M. G. Coy.	via RAIMBERT - BURBURE.
No.3 Co. Div. Train.	via BURBURE.
1/6th London Brigade, R.F.A.	via RAIMBERT - BURBURE.
1/6th Lon. Fld Ambce.	via HAUT RIEUX (after 13th London Battery RFA has passed cross roads C.12.a.6.3.)
Troops from HURIONVILLE.	via road through U.21.a. and U.15.d.
1/5th Lon. Fld Ambce.	via RAIMBERT - BURBURE.
H.Q. & H.Q.Co. Train.	via BURBURE.
Section of D.A.C.	via RAIMBERT - BURBURE.

ROUTE for movement of TROOPS ENTRAINING AT FOUQUEREUIL.

Troops from ALLOUAGNE.	via LE REVEILLON - CHOCQUES - Cross roads D.6.a.9.9. - Cross roads E.7.c.6.4. - FOUQUEREUIL.
No.4 Co. Div. Train.	via AUCHEL - MARLES - LAPUGNOY - LABEUVRIERE.
Troops from BURBURE.	via road junction C.12.a.6.2., thence as above.
Troops from LAPUGNOY.	via LABEUVRIERE.
1/8th Lon.Bde, R.F.A.	CAUCHY - AUCHEL - MARLES - LAPUGNOY - LABEUVRIERE.
4th Bn. R. Welsh Fsrs.	LAPUGNOY - LABEUVRIERE.
D. A. C.	MARLES - LAPUGNOY - LABEUVRIERE.

Hdqrtrs, 47th Divn.
15th Feb.1916.
S/107.

Lieut.Colonel,
A.A. & Q.M.G., 47th (London) Division.

SECRET.

Headquarters,
140th Infantry Brigade.

Reference S/107 dated 15-2-16, the following additional instructions are issued.

(1) Every unit will entrain with the current day's and the next day's rations and forage.

To ensure this, all units entraining between midnight and the customary hour of refilling will need to draw a day's rations

This will be arranged for as follows:

O.C. Supply Column will have one day's supplies for each train load of troops at the entraining station two hours before the time of departure of train, and will bring sufficient loaders to railhead to load up supplies on to the train. O.C. units will detail a representative to take over these supplies two hours before the time of departure of their train.

(2) The following to be on duty as entraining officers:

Major WHITEHEAD,
    6th Bn. London Regt. ... ... BERGUETTE.

Capt. WARD,
    19th Bn. " " ... ... LILLERS.

Capt. BARE,
    22nd Bn. " " ... ... FOUQUEREUIL.

Hdqrtrs,　　　　　　　　　　　(sd) S.Thunder,
47th Div.　　　　　　　　　　　Lieut. Colonel,
S/107/7.　　　　　　A.A. & Q.M.G., 47th (London) Division.
17/2/16.

(2)

Officer Commanding,
    8th Bn. London Regiment.

For information and necessary action.

C/541
18/2/1916.
　　　　　　　　　　　　　　　　　Captain,
　　　　　　　　　　　　　　　Brigade Major,
　　　　　　　　　　　　　　140th Infantry Brigade.

257

SECRET.

Officer Commanding
    8th Bn. London Regiment.

        The Brigade will be held at the usual three hours
readiness although they are in G.H.Q. Reserve; as there is the
possibility, in case of active operations on the IVth Corps
front, the Division might be placed at the disposal of that
Corps.
        In this contingency transport could move by road, and a
guard could be placed on stores until arrival of train

                                        Captain,
                                     Brigade Major,
                                  140th Infantry Brigade.

BRIGADE OFFICE No. C/5742 18 FEB. 1916 140TH INFANTRY BRIGADE

Vertical and Oblique Photographs & portion of Sheet 44 (1:20,000) showing Area Covered.

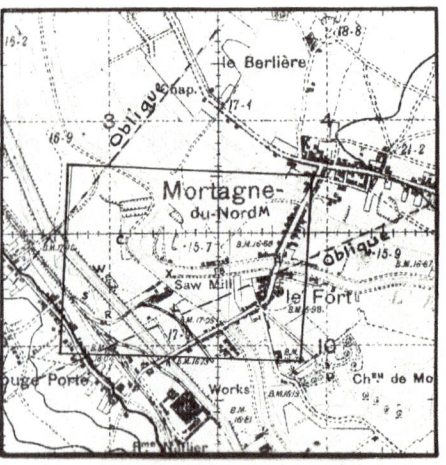

B.I.S.

Army Form C. 2118

8th London Regt:
Post Off'd Rifles.

WAR DIARY
INTELLIGENCE SUMMARY

March 1916.

(Erase heading not required.)

Instructions regarding War Diaries and Intelligence Summaries are contained in F.S. Regs., Part II. and the Staff Manual respectively. Title Pages will be prepared in manuscript.

Place	Date March	Hour	Summary of Events and Information	Remarks and references to Appendices
Bomy	1-3	—	Bn. remained at Bomy and took part in Brigade training operations	
Reclinghem	4	—	Bn. left Bomy at 1 p.m. & went to Reclinghem	
"	4-8	—	Bn. remained at Reclinghem and continued Brigade training.	
Fiefs	9	—	Bn. left Reclinghem and marched to Fiefs & went into billets there; part of Divisional march.	
Ourton	10	—	" " Fiefs " " Ourton " " " " " Bn. marched as a Battalion.	
"	11-15	—	" remained at Ourton.	
Gouy-Servins	16	—	" left Ourton and marched to Gouy-Servins & went into billets, taking over from 1st Worcester Regt.; the 47th Division relieving the 23rd Division; & the 140th Bde coming into support.	
"	17-20	—	Bn. remained at Gouy-Servins, providing working parties by night. 9 o.r. joined the Bn. from the base on the 19th.	
"	21	—	Bn. left Gouy-Servins and marched to Villers au Bois arriving 2 p.m.; left Villers au Bois at 7 p.m. and relieved 20th London Regt: in front line trenches, Right Sub-Section.	
Trenches	22-26	—	Bn. remained in trenches. 1 o.r. killed 22nd 1 o.r. wounded 25th	
Estrée-Cauchie	27	—	Bn. was relieved by 23rd Londn Regt: & leaving trenches shortly before midnight marched to Estrée-Cauchie; the Brigade coming into Reserve. 1 o.r. wounded.	
"	28-31	—	Bn. remained at Estrée-Cauchie. 29th 9 o.r. joined Bn. from base.	

B D Vine Capt:
O.C. 8th London Regt:
1st April 1916.

SECRET.

140th INFANTRY BRIGADE ORDER No.88.   Copy No.

Reference.   8th March, 1916.

1/100,000 HAZEBROUCK 5a & LENS 11.

1. 140th and 141st Infantry Brigades will move tomorrow, 141st Brigade leading. 140th Brigade will move in accordance with attached march table, and will march on BINET via MERVILLE-NEDONCHELLE.

2. Units will only remain one night in new billets.

3. 1st line transport will follow their own units until reaching starting point when they will be brigaded in the same order as their own units. A half Company will follow the transport of each Battalion.

4. Billeting parties will march at the head of the Brigade and should be provided with cycles. They will report to the Brigade Major after the column passes the 8th Battalion starting point.

5. Refilling point will be at AUCHY AU BOIS cross roads at 12 noon.

6. Instructions for lorries are being issued separately.

7. Brigade Headquarters will close at DELETTE at 9 a.m. and will reopen on arrival in the new billeting area.

                                        [signature]   Captain,
                                                      Brigade Major,
Issued at   140th Infantry Brigade.

Copy No. 1. War Diary.
         2. File.
         3. 47th Division. (By Signal Service)
         4. 6th Battn.   ,,
         5. 7th   ,,   ,,
         6. 8th   ,,   ,,
         7. 15th   ,,   ,,
         8. Machine Gun Coy.   ,,
         9. Transport Officer.   ,,
        10. Detachment 4th Field Amb.   ,,
        11. No.3 Coy. 47th Div. Train.   ,,
        12. 141st Inf. Bde.   ,,
        13. Spare.
        14.   ,,
        15.   ,,

213

MARCH TABLE.

UNIT.	STARTING POINT.	TIME.	ROUTE TO CANAL'S BILLETING POINT. AREA.	REMARKS.
Brigade Headqrs.	Five Lane Ends.	9.35 a.m.	BELLEVUE - TRIX Road.	
6th Battalion.	do.	9.36 a.m.	do.	
15th do.	do.	9.39 a.m.	COYECOUT - Pt.140 Road.	(15th Bn. will not pass fork road (i.e. of Pt.140 until the 6th Bn. have passed.
7th do.	do.	9.42 a.m.	Direct road from MERCUARIE to Five Lane Ends.Transport via BELLEVE. via BOIS.	
8th do.	Cross roads 300 yds. S.W. of S in HUY ST JULIEN.	10.0 a.m.		(8th Bn. will not pass their starting point until the 7th Bn. have passed. They will not pass Battn. of 141st Bde. at boi. M.G.Coy will follow 7th Bn. until the starting point of 8th Bn. when it will halt to allow 8th Bn. to come in.
140th M.G.Coy.	Five Lane Ends.	9.45 a.m.	COYECOUT - Pt.140 Road.	
Sect No.4 Fld.Amb.	do.	9.47 a.m.	Direct road from THEROUANNE to Five Lane Ends.	
1st line transport.				
No.2 Coy.Div.Train. (less supply wagons)				(Will follow 7th Bn. transport until arrival at starting point of 8th Bn. when it will halt to allow 8th Bn. Tmspt to come in.

Units will be informed of new Billeting area during the march.

214

SECRET.   Copy No. ..6..

140th INFANTRY BRIGADE ORDER NO. 66.

                                                                  9.3.16.

Reference.
Sheet 36 b. 1/40,000.

1.   The 140th Infantry Brigade will move tomorrow in accordance with attached March table.

2.   1st line transport will march with their own units.

3.   Billeting parties will leave their present billets at 8.30 a.m. and will meet Staff Captain at OURTON Church at 10 a.m. and at DIVION at 10.30 a.m. The 7th Battn. billeting party will proceed direct to BEUGIN.

4.   Separate instructions are being issued about lorries.

5.   Brigade Headquarters will close at FIEFS at 10.30 a.m. and will reopen on arrival at the Brewery, DIVION.

                                                    Captain,
                                                    Brigade Major,
                                                    140th Infantry Brigade.

Issued at

Copy No. 1 War Diary.
        2 File.
        3 47th Division.   By Signal Section.
        4 6th Battalion.   do.
        5 7th   do.   do.
        6 8th   do.   do.
        7 15th do.   do.
        8 Machine Gun Coy.   do.
        9 Bde. Transport Officer.   do.
       10 Detachmt. No.4 Fld.Amb.   do.
       11 No. 2 Coy. Div. Train.   do.
       12 SignalCoy. No.4 Section.
       13. Spare.
       14. ,,
       15. ,,

MARCH TABLE.

UNIT.	STARTING POINTS.	TIME.	ROUTE.	NEW BILLETING AREA.	REMARKS.
Brigade Headers.	FIEFS.	11.0 a.m. via PERNES-GAMBLAIN CHATELAIN.		DIVION.	
6th Battalion.	AMETTES.	11.0 a.m. via FERFAY - CAUCHY LA TOUR.		DIVION.	
7th do.	FONTAINE.	11.20 a.m. via BAILLEUL LES PERNES - PERNES -OURTON.		BEUGIN.	
8th do.	FIEFS.	11.5 a.m. via PERNES.		OURTON.	
15th do.	NEDON.	11.0 a.m. via AMETTES - FERFAY - CAUCHY LA TOUR.		DIVION.	
140th M.G.Coy.	NEDONCHELLE.	11.25 a.m. via BAILLEUL LES PERNES - PERNES.		OURTON.	Follow 7th Bn.
4th Lond.Fld.Amb.	FIEFS.	11.15 a.m. via PERNES.- GAMBLAIN CHATELAIN - DIVION.		BRUAY.	
No. 2 Coy. Div. Train.	-	-		DIVION.	Train will march with its own units.

NOTE. Billets and horse standings near DIVION on both sides of BRUAY - DIVION Road East of cross roads J.19.c.0.9. are allotted to 47th Divisional Train.

4th Corps No.H.R.S.ER610.

4th Corps.

Reference 1st Army No. G.S. 236, dated 15/12/15.

Several cases have occurred recently when, although the daily ammunition return has shewn a considerable expenditure by a corps, there has been nothing in the morning or evening situation of the Corps concerned to shew that any bombardment of the enemy's positions has taken place.

2. The morning and evening situation reports are invariably to refer to all artillery operations which may have necessitated an abnormal expenditure of ammunition.

G.S.220
5/3/16.

(sd) G.de S. Barrow, Maj.Genl.
General Staff,
1st Army.

(2)

140th Infantry Brigade.

For information, necessary action in future, and retention.

G/875.
7/3/16.

(sd) A.W.Webber, Major,
General Staff,
47th (London) Division.

(3)

Officer Commanding,
   8th Bn. London Regiment.

For information.

Captain,
Brigade Major,
140th Infantry Brigade.

261

London Regt.

125 Spare Copy   SECRET.

The following is the order of urgency in which work on this Brigade Frontage will be taken up; no other work is to be attempted:-

1. Before any serious work can be done in the Front Line the Communication trenches must be cleaned and made passable for the carriage of Stores. This will be done by "picking" up the trench boards, cleaning out the trench below - scraping the boards and replacing them.
   The following main avenues of approach only will be treated in this way at present:-

Trench	Battn. responsible.
1. BOY. COBURG.-	19th Battn.
2. BOY.DU CHEMIN CREUX-)	
3. BOY.PELLETIER -)	"C" Battn.

Working parties will be detailed for this by Battns. responsible as above and carried out by day.

2. Selected portions of the Front Line trench must be "developed" the passage behind the firestep being deepened - parapet raised and a firestep left and revetted as follows:-

   1st. The trench boarding will be picked up and scraped clean.
   2nd. The trench must be dug out below the trench boarding to a depth of at least $6\frac{1}{4}'$ below the top of the parapet and a width of 24", taking care to leave an 18" firestep, as follows:-

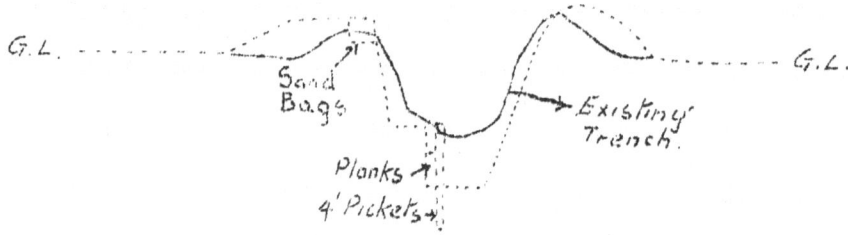

   3rd. Trench boards must be replaced and the parapet built up and revetted with sandbags; where, owing to the swampy state of the ground, digging and deepening of the trench is impossible, the parapet must be raised and a breastwork constructed of sandbags using several thousand daily.

   4th. The firestep must be revetted with planks and pickets and, if necessary, built up and made secure.

Instead of attempting to develop the whole front line, special points should be selected and tackled in short lengths: the points to be selected should preferably be round the heads of Communication trenches, with the object of eventually forming strong points round the heads of these Communications and also in portions of the line giving good flanking fire etc.
   The following will be required:-
   (a) Tools.- Picks, Shovels, Mudscoops and Scrapers, mauls and a few saws.
   (b) Material. New trench boards, Sandbags(several thousand per Battn.daily) 4' pickets (with wire bound heads) and planks.

Commanding Officers will inform Brigade H.Q. by wire immediately what quantities of the above will be required daily.
   The above is all that can be attempted immediately. The bulk of the work can be done by day and must be carried out by platoons holding the Front Line continuously without ceasing until completed.
   Attention is drawn to the following extracts from a memorandum

Spare Copy

recently published by the Commander-in-Chief:-

" With the approach of finer weather, and consequently increased intensity in fighting, the time has now come for every man to put forth his utmost efforts. Commanders must not rest satisfied with merely "a fair days work", but must insist on the utmost possible effort from now onwards."

The Brigadier General Commanding feels confident that the Brigade will respond to this appeal and strain every nerve to alter the present unsatisfactory state of affairs.

Later on the following programme will be carried out :-
(a) Traverses built in the fire trench.
(b) Close Support Line deepened and developed as above.
(c) Other Communication trenches developed.
(d) Reserve Line deepened and developed as above.
(e) Dug-outs prepared.
(f) Front Line Wire strengthened.

3. Sufficient copies of this are forwarded for distribution to Company Commanders.

B.M.S. 39.
15/3/16.

(sd) B.Battye, Major,
Brigade Major,
141st Inf.Bde.

(2)

140th Inf.Bde.
================

The attached Secret Memo No.B.M.S.39, dated 15th March, 1916, of 141st Inf.Bde. is passed for information in order that the work may be continuous as reliefs take place.

G/863/25.
17/3/16.

(sd) A.W.Webber, Major,
General Staff,
47th (London) Division.

(3)

Officer Commanding,

For information and distribution to all Company Commanders.

JBCarlisle.
Lieut.
for Brigade Major,
140th Infantry Brigade.

SCHEDULE.

Unit.	Unit of 142nd Bde. Relieving.	Unit of 141st Bde. Relieved.	Sub-section.	Date.	Guides. Place.	Time.	Remarks.
(C) 6th Battn.	24th Battn.	19th Bn.	(Reserve (Centre.	20th March.	Cross roads X.16.c.3.3.	7.30 p.m.	
7th "	21st "	17th Bn.	Left.	Night 21/22 Mch. Night 20/21 Mch.	Sugar Factory.	1.0 a.m.	
(A) 8th "	23rd "	20th Bn.	Right.	Night 21/22 Mch.	Cross roads X.16.c.3.3.	8.30 p.m.	
(B) 15th " (C)	24th " "	—	Reserve.	Night 21/22 Mch.	—	—	(H.Q.2 Coys (CARENCY (2 Coys. (VILLERS AU (BOIS.
140th M.G.Coy.	142nd M.G.Coy.	141st M.G.Coy.	Trenches.	Arrangements for relief of machine guns to be made direct between M.G.Coy.Commanders.			
140/1 T.M.B.	—	—	Right.		Cross roads X.16.c.3.3.	8.0 p.m.	
140/2 T.M.B.	—	—	Left.		do.	8.0 p.m.	

(A) The 8th Battn. moves into VILLERS AU BOIS at 2 p.m. 21st March and carries out relief of right sub-section in evening.
(B) The 15th Battn. will send guides to old Bde H.Q. ABLAIN ST.NAZAIRE at 7.30 p.m.
(C) 6th and 15th Bns. will send billoting parties to CARENCY and VILLERS AU BOIS on morning March 20th and 21st March respectively.

SECRET.

Copy No. 6

140th INFANTRY BRIGADE ORDER No. 69.

25th March, 1916.

1. The 140th Infantry Brigade will be relieved by the 142nd Infantry Brigade on 26th and 27th March, 1916.

2. Reliefs will be carried out in accordance with attached Schedule.

3. Receipts will be taken for all trench stores, and copies forwarded to Brigade Headquarters by 6 p.m., 28th March, 1916.

4. Brigade Headquarters will close at VILLERS AU BOIS on 27th at 4.30 p.m., and will re-open on arrival at FRESNICOURT.

Issued at 4.15 p.m.

R.V. Foster Captain,
Brigade Major,
140th Infantry Brigade.

```
Copy No.  1   File
    ,,    2   War Diary
    ,,    3   47th Div.           By Sig.Sec.
    ,,    4   6th Bn.Lond.Regt.       ,,
    ,,    5   7th Bn.    ,,           ,,
    ,,    6   8th        ,,           ,,
    ,,    7   15th       ,,           ,,
    ,,    8    Bde.M.G.Coy.           ,,
    ,,    9   140/1 T.M.B.            ,,
    ,,   10   140/2 T.M.B.            ,,
    ,,   11   Bde.Gren.Offr.          ,,
    ,,   12   Bde.Trans.Offr.         ,,
    ,,   13   Bde.Ammn.Res.Offr.      ,,
    ,,   14   142 Inf.Bde.            ,,
    ,,   15   141    ,,               ,,
    ,,   16   138    ,,               ,,
    ,,   17   24     ,,               ,,
    ,,   18   1/3rd R.E.              ,,
    ,,   19   2/3rd R.E.              ,,
    ,,   20   No.4 Sig.Sec.
    ,,   21   Spare
    ,,   22    ,,
    ,,   23    ,,
```

SECRET.   Copy No...6

140th INFANTRY BRIGADE ORDER NO. 67.

Ref. Sheets. 36 b & c 1/40,000.

1. The 47th Division is relieving the 23rd Division in the Right (CARENCY) Sector of the 4th Corps Front.

2. The Brigade will move in accordance with attached March table. All day reliefs to be completed by 12 noon.

3. O.C. 15th Bn. will proceed with the G.O.C. Brigade to reconnoitre LORETTE Support trenches on March 14th.

4. The G.O.C. 140th Brigade will take over command on March 16th at 12 noon. Until then units in new area will be under command of G.O.C. 69th Brigade.

5. Units will leave present billets at 8 a.m.

6. Separate instructions will be issued for lorries.

7. Brigade Headquarters will remain at DIVION until March 16th, when they will move to a place to be notified later.

                                            R.J. Foster, Captain,
                                                    Brigade Major,
                                                140th Infantry Brigade.

Issued at ....

Copy No. 1. War Diary.
        2. File.
        3. 47th Division.   By Signal Section.
        4. 6th Bn. London Regt.   ,,
        5. 7th   do.   ,,
        6. 8th   do.   ,,
        7. 15th   do.   ,,
        8. Machine Gun Coy.   ,,
        9. Transport Officer.   ,,
       10. 69th Inf. Bde.   ,,
       11. O.C. No.2 Coy. Div. Train.   ,,
       12. Supply Officer, 140th Bde.   ,,
       13. Bde. Amm. Res. Officer.   ,,
       14. No.4 Sect. Signal Coy.   ,,
       15. xxxxxxxx 24th Brigade   ,,
       16. ,,
       17. ,,

TABLE OF MOVES.

Date.	Unit of 140th Inf.Bde.	From.	Unit relieved.	New billets.	Remarks.
March					
i. Day 13th.	15th Bn. London Regt. 1 Sect. Machine Gun Coy.	DIVION. OURTON.	C Bn. 69th InfBde.	BOUVIGNY HUTS. R.25.a.	
ii. Night 14/15.	15th Bn. London Regt. 1.Sect.Machine Gun Coy.	BOUVIGNY HUTS.	D Bn. 69th Inf.Bde.	LORETTE Support trenches.	
iii. Day 15th.	6th Bn.London Regt. 1 Sect.M.G.Coy.	DIVION. OURTON.	D Bn. 69th Inf.Bde.	BOUVIGNY HUTS.	
iv. Day 16th.	7th Bn.London Regt. 8th do. M.G.Coy. less 2 sections.	BEUGIN. OURTON. OURTON.	B Bn. 24th Inf.Bde. C Bn. 24th Inf.Bde.	VILLERS AU BOIS. LES SERVINS. LES SERVINS.	

222

SECRET.   Copy No.....

140th INFANTRY BRIGADE ORDER No. 68.

Reference.   19/3/16.
  56b = c.1/40,000.

1.   The 140th Infantry Brigade will relieve the 141st Infantry Brigade in Front line and the 142nd Infantry Brigade will come into support.

2.   Moves will take place in accordance with attached schedule.

3.   Receipt will be given for all trench stores and copies sent to this office by 9 a.m. on 22nd March.

4.   Brigade Headquarters will close at GOUY SERVINS at 4 p.m. on 21st March, and will reopen on arrival at VILLERS AU BOIS.

Issued at........   R V Foster
                                              Captain,
                                              Brigade Major,
                                              140th Infantry Brigade.

Copy No. 1. Operation Order File.
         2. War Diary.
         3. 47th Division.   By Signal Section.
         4. 6th Bn. London Regt.   ,,
         5. 7th   ,,   ,,
         6. 8th   ,,   ,,
         7. 15th   ,,   ,,
         8. Machine Gun Coy.   ,,
         9. Bde.Transport Officer.   ,,
        10. No.4 Sect.Signals.   ,,
        11. 142nd Inf.Bde.   ,,
        12. 140/1 T...Bty.   ,,
        13. 140/2 T...Bty.   ,,
        14. Bde.Amm.Res.Officer.   ,,
        15. Bde.Grenadier Officer.   ,,
        16. Spare.
        17.   ,,
        18.   ,,

SECRET.   Copy No. 6

140th BRIGADE ORDER No. 70.

31st March, 1916.

Reference - Sheets 36B & C, 1-40000th.

1. The 140th Infantry Brigade will relieve the 141st Infantry Brigade in Support, in accordance with attached Schedule, on 1st and 2nd April, 1916.

2. Officer Commanding, 7th Bn. London Regiment will give a receipt for all stores taken over in the LORETTE Trenches, and send a copy to Brigade Headquarters by 6 p.m. on 3rd April, 1916.

3. Brigade Machine Gun Company will remain at GOUY SERVINS.

4. 140/1 and 140/2 Trench Mortar Batteries will remain with 6th Bn. London Regiment.

5. Brigade Headquarters close at FRESNICOURT at 3.30 p.m. on 2nd April, 1916, and will re-open on arrival at GOUY SERVINS.

R.V. Foster
Captain,
Brigade Major,
140th Infantry Brigade.

Copy No.		
1	File.	
2	War Diary.	
3	47th Div.	By Sig. Sec.
4	6th Lond. Regt.	,,
5	7th do.	,,
6	8th do.	,,
7	15th do.	,,
8	Bde. M.G. Coy.	,,
9	Bde. Ammn. Reserve Offr.	,,
10	Bde. Grenadier Offr.	,,
11	Bde. Transport Offr.	,,
12	140/1 T.M.B.	,,
13	140/2 do.	,,
14	141st Inf. Brigade	,,
15	142nd do.	,,
16	No. 4 Section Sigs.	,,
17	Spare	
18	do.	
19	do.	

SCHEDULE.

Unit	Relieving Unit	Date	Sub-Section	Guides Place	Time	New Billeting Area	Remarks
6th Lond. Regt.	22nd Lond. Regt.	Night 27/28th	Centre	Cross Roads X.16.c.3.3.	7.45 p.m. 8-30	MAISNIL BOUCHEE	
7th do.	21st do. 23rd do.	(Night 26/27th) 27th	Left	Sugar Factory.	1.0 a.m.	VILLERS AU BOIS VERDREL	23rd Lond. Regt. arrives about 2 p.m.
(1) 8th do.	23rd do.	Night 27/28th	Right	CABARET ROUGE.	8.30 p.m. 7-45 p.m	ESTREE CAUCHIE	
15th do.	22nd do.	26th 27th	Reserve -----			VERDREL FRESNICOURT	22nd Lond. Regt. will arrive about 12.30 p.m. 15th Lond. Regt. will arrive at FRESNICOURT at 4 p.m.
M.G. Coy.	142nd M.G.Coy.	26th 27th	-----			GOUY SERVINS	Arrangements to be made by Bde. M.G. Officers direct.
140/1 T.M.B.	142/1 T.M.B.	Night 27/28th	Right	CABARET ROUGE.	8.30 p.m.	MAISNIL, BOUCHEE	
140/2 T.M.B.	142/2 T.M.B.	Night 27/28th	Centre	X.16.c.3.3.	7.45 p.m. 8.30	MAISNIL BOUCHEE	

(1) Via VILLERS AU BOIS - ST. ELOI Road - DUCK WALK and BOYAU DE LA REDOUTE to and from CABARET ROUGE.

MARCH TABLE.

Unit.	Time to pass starting point. Railway Crossing over LILLERS-ST HILAIRE Rd. just N. of S. in LILLERS.	Billeting area.	Point to leave column.	Remarks.
140th Inf.Bde. Hdqrs.	—	BRAY-ST-JULIEN.	—	
8th Lond.Regt.	8.45 a.m.	BOMY.	Cross roads at J. in BRAY-ST-JULIEN.	
15th do.	8.50 a.m.	BRAY-ST-JULIEN.	—	
8th do.	8.55 a.m.	ENQUIN-LES-MINES.	CUHEM.	
7th do.	9.0 a.m.	ENGUINGATTE.	Cross roads just north of pt 96 about 900 yds W of R. in NELY.	
140th Bde. M.Gun Coy.	9.5 a.m.	RUPTIGNY.	Cross roads at J. in BRAY-ST-JULIEN.	
Sect. 4th Lond. Field Amb.	9.8 a.m.	ENQUIN-LES-MINES.	CUHEM.	
1st Line Trnprt. (Brigaded)	9.10 a.m.	—	—	1st Line Transport Baggage wagons will leave the column at same points as are laid down for their units.
No.2 Coy.Div. Train. (Supply only)	9.30 a.m.	ENGUINGATTE.	—	

228

SECRET

140th Infantry Brigade.

The 47th Division will be called on to furnish large working parties for work on back lines and trench tramways in the new areas: technical supervision being supplied by 4th Corps.

The following extract from 4th Corps letter on this subject is forwarded for the information of all concerned.

" Infantry officers are responsible for distributing their men on the work, that their men work properly, and that the instructions given by the R.E. are carried out.

The R.E. are responsible for guiding the parties to the work, for issuing tools, for explaining the work to be done to the officer in charge and for general supervision.

Any failure of a party to work properly is to be reported to the C.E., 4th Corps. "

G/863/TM7.
6/3/16.

(sd) N.W.Webber, Major,
General Staff,
46th (London) Division.

(S)

Officer Commanding,
8th Bn. London Regiment.

For information.

Captain,
Brigade Major,
140th Infantry Brigade.

BRIGADE OFFICE
No. S/13
7 - MAR 1916
140th INFANTRY BRIGADE

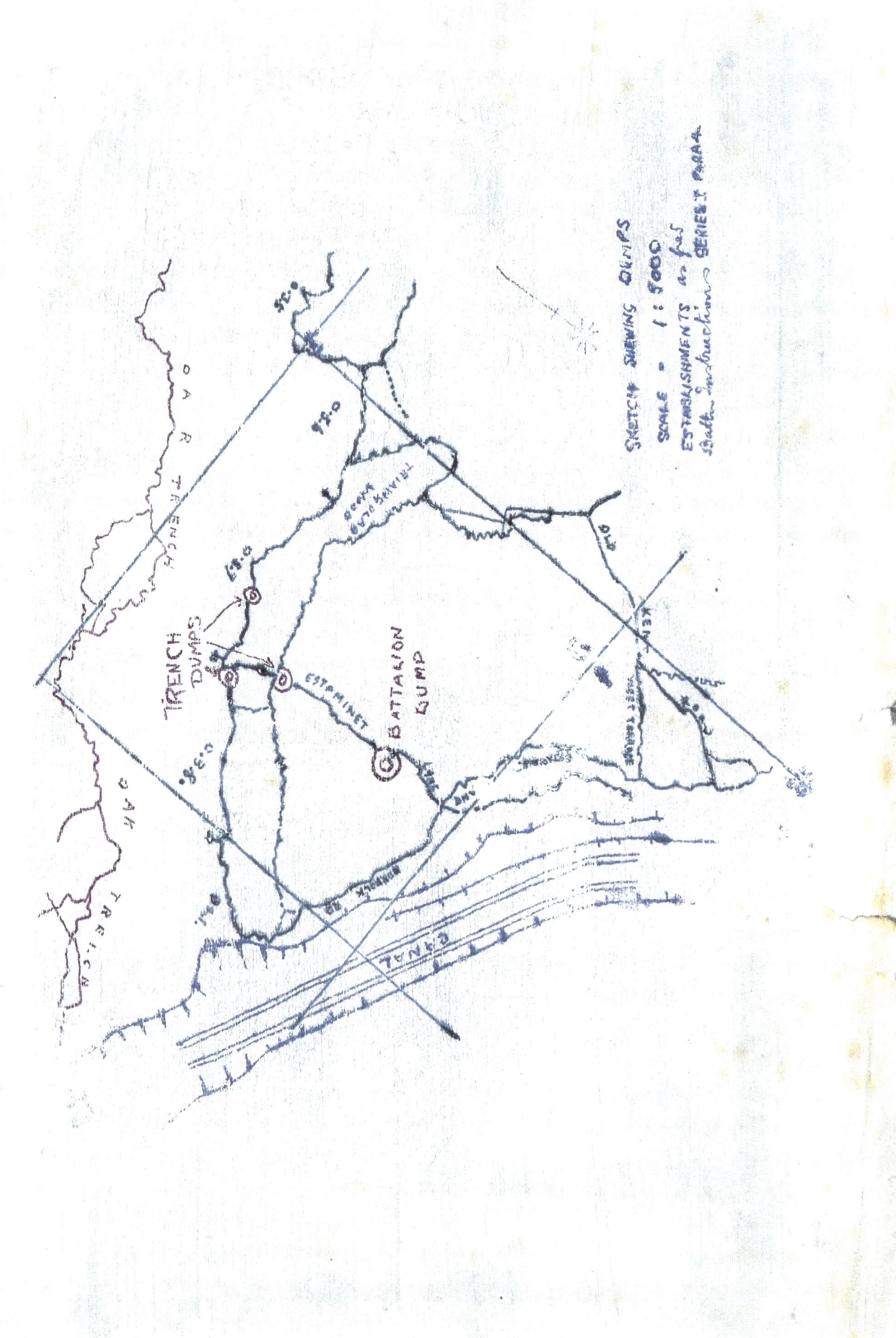

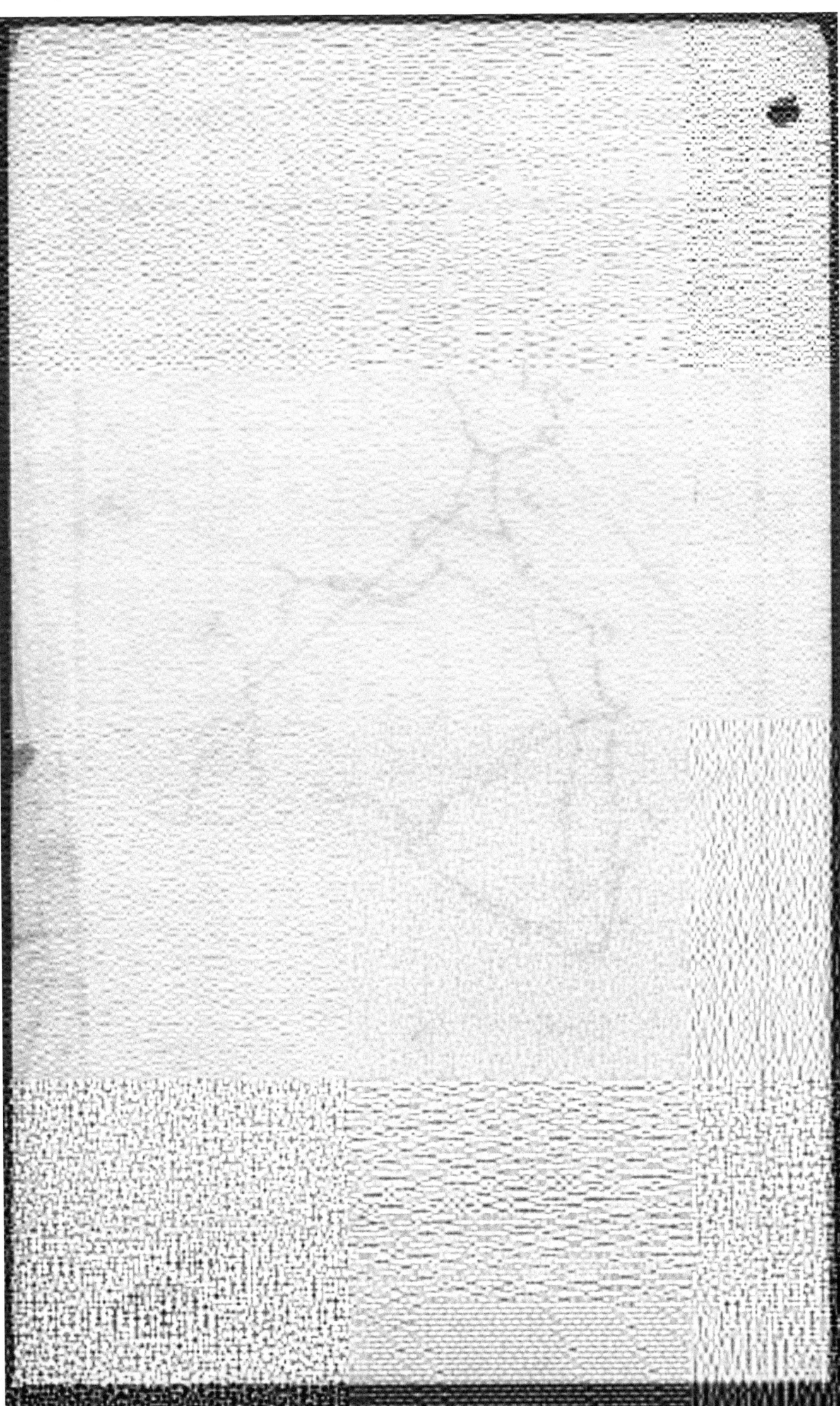

Issued 9.15 am.
Copy 1: 1/2nd Lon. B^n
     2 Civilian
     to all concerned

8th London Regt:
(Post Office Rifles)

Copy No 2

Operation Order No 7
by Captain W.B. Vince

Reference — France, Sheets 36ᵇ S.E, 6ᵗʰ Edᵗⁿ
and 36ᵃ S.W, 6ᵗʰ Edᵗⁿ — 1/20,000.

1). The Bⁿ will be relieved to-night by 21st London Regt.

2). Platoon guides, & guides for bombers & Lewis gun, will parade at Bⁿ Hqrs at 7.20 p.m. and will proceed to CABARET ROUGE under 2.Lt. Potter.

3). Coys will move out independently on relief and proceed via ERSATZ — BOYAU CABARET ROUGE — X roads X 16 d 94 — CARENCY — new road in X 14 & 13 to VERDREL.

4) Cookers, & carts for new packs & chargers, will meet Coys on new road just beyond CARENCY.

5). Very pistols, periscopes (except the two HARP pattern), & steel helmets will be taken out. Trench stores will be handed over & receipts taken — Certificates of cleanliness will also be obtained — Receipts & certificates to reach O.R. by 9 am to-morrow.

6) Lewis gun limber will be at ration dump at 9.30 p.m.

7) O.C. Coys, Billeting Officer & L.G. Officer of 21st Bⁿ will arrive in advance of Bⁿ (about 4-15) — Weed.
Capt & Adjt
8th Lon. Regt.

"A" Form.
MESSAGES AND SIGNALS.

Army Form C. 2121.

No. of Message _____

| Prefix ____ Code ____ m. | Words | Charge | This message is on a/c of: | Recd. at ____ |
| Office of Origin and Service Instructions. | Sent At ____ m. To ____ By ____ | | _____ Service. (Signature of "Franking Officer.") | Date ____ From ____ By ____ |

TO {

*	Sender's Number.	Day of Month	In reply to Number	**A A A**

232

From ____
Place ____
Time ____

The above may be forwarded as now corrected. (Z)

Censor. Signature of Addressor or person authorised to telegraph in his name.

* This line should be erased if not required.

(4198) Wt. W14042—M44. 300000 Pads. 12/15. Sir J. C. & S.

6th.

Headquarters,
140th Infantry Brigade.

Dispositions.

Left Coy. B Coy.   1 Platoon and 1 Lewis Gun in shell holes
                    from J.8.a.6.6 to J.8.a.8.3.
                    1 Platoon in segments of trench in
                    JABBER SUPPORT, J.8.a.1.4 to J.8.a.4.9
                    2 Platoons and 1 Lewis Gun in JABBER Tr.
                    J.7.b.7.2 to J.8.c.0.9.

Right Coy. D Coy.   1 Platoon in old gun position and shell
                    holes at about J.8.c.9.9.
                    3 Platoons in JABBER SUPPORT, J.8.c.4.9 -
                    J.8.c.5.2.

Support Coy. C Coy. 2 Platoons JABBER Tr. from J.8.c.2.4 to
                    J.8.c.2.2 approx.
                    2 Platoons JABBER DRIVE, J.8.c.2.4 to
                    J.8.c.0.6 approx.

233

Secret   113.

Copy No. 6.

140th Infantry Brigade Order No.64.

(Ref. BAKERHOUSE, 5A 1/100,000).

7.7.1916.

1. The 140th Infantry Brigade with Section 4th London Field Ambulance will move into new billets in the NINING area tomorrow.

2. Units will move independently to billets as in attached schedule.

3. Units will leave their present billets at 11 a.m.

4. Billeting parties will leave present billets at 9 p.m.

5. Instructions as to baggage wagons and lorries will be sent when received.

6. Refilling point will remain as at present.

7. Brigade Headquarters will close at CAMP ST.JULIEN at 11 a.m. and will reopen at BLETTE on arrival.

M Foster
Captain.
Brigade Major,
140th Infantry Brigade.

Issued at 10.15

Copy No. 1. War Diary.
 ,,   ,, 2. File.
 ,,   ,, 3. 47th Division.   By Signal Service.
 ,,   ,, 4. 6th Bn.Lon.Regt.   ,,
 ,,   ,, 5. 7th   ,,   ,,
 ,,   ,, 6. 8th   ,,   ,,
 ,,   ,, 7. 15th   ,,   ,,
 ,,   ,, 8. Machine Gun Company.   ,,
 ,,   ,, 9. Transport Officer.   ,,
 ,,   ,, 10. 4th Field Ambulance   ,,
 ,,   ,, 11. No.2 Coy.47th Div.Train.   ,,
 ,,   ,, 12. Spare.   ,,
 ,,   ,, 13.   ,,   ,,

UNIT.	NEW BILLETING AREA.
Brigade Headquarters	DILETTE.
6th Battalion.	do.
7th do.	THIEMBRONNE.
8th do.	RECLINGHEM.
10th do.	COYECQUE.
140 Machine Gun Coy.	do.
Section 4th Lon.Field Ambce.	BIMLLES.

260

140th Infantry Brigade.

   Reference G/841/2 dated 7/3/16.
   The demonstration will be held at K.19.a.5.9 at 11.30 a.m. on March 15th.
   Units will make their own arrangements to send their parties to the demonstration.
   No transport can be provided.

G/841/2/1.   (sd.) H.R.TESSER, Major,
10th March 1916.   47th (London) Division.

2.

Officer Commanding,
  8th Lon. Regt.

   For information with reference to my 5/17, dated 7th March, 1916.

                Captain,
              Brigade Major,
            140th Infantry Brigade.

264

8 London Regt.

Vol XIV

April 1916

234

SECRET.   IVth Corps.No.H.R.S.684.
           First Army No.G.S.344
           47th Div. No.G/1023.

IVth Corps.

It is reported that during the recent fighting at VERDUN, the Germans have made much use of gas shells. These were used against the ground behind the trenches rather than against the trenches themselves. So many were fired into woods, valleys, etc., behind the French lines, it is said, that gas helmets had to be worn by artillery personnel, commanders and staffs, etc., constantly, day and night.

                (s) S.H. WILSON, Lt.Col.
First Army.   General Staff, for Major General,
14/4/16.   General Staff, 1st Army.

                    (2)

Officer Commanding,
     8th Bn. London Regt.

            For information.

                                for Captain,
                                     Brigade Major,
                                     140th Infantry Brigade.

235

Army Form C. 2118

8th London Regt.
(Post Office Rifles)

WAR DIARY
INTELLIGENCE SUMMARY
April 1916

(Erase heading not required.)

Instructions regarding War Diaries and Intelligence Summaries are contained in F.S. Regs, Part II. and the Staff Manual respectively. Title Pages will be prepared in manuscript.

Place	Date	Hour	Summary of Events and Information	Remarks and references to Appendices
Estrée-Cauchie	April 1	-	Bn. remained in billets at Estrée-Cauchie.	
Gouy-Servins	2	-	The Bn. coming into support, the Bn. moved into billets at Gouy-Servins.	
"	3-7	-	Bn. remained at Gouy-Servins.	
Villers-au-Bois	8	-	Bn. going into the line, Bn. moved from Gouy at 1 a.m. to Villers-au-Bois, & at 6.30 p.m. into A sub-section, Carency sector.	
A sub-section Carency Sector		-	Bn. billets inspected by G.O.C. Div. 1 Officer & 120 O.R. detached for permanent working party & billeted at Villers-au-Bois.	
"	9-13	-	Bn. remained in A sub-section - Casualties :- O.R. killed 3, wounded 7, died of wounds 2.	
Verdrel	14	-	Bn. going into reserve, Bn. was relieved by 21st London Regt. & proceeded to billets at Verdrel.	
"	15-18	-	Bn. remained at Verdrel. On 16th a reinforcement of 22 O.R. joined. On 17th Bn. was inspected by & marched past G.O.C. Div.	
Bouvigny Huts	19	-	Bn. relieved 19th London Regt. in Bouvigny Huts, taking over at 11 a.m.	
Lorette Trenches	20	-	Bn. coming into support, Bn. relieved 20th Bn. in support trenches in Lorette Ridge. Bn. Hqrs. at Ablain St Nazaire.	
"	20-25	-	Bn. remained in Lorette Trenches 23rd 1 O.T. wounded.	
Villers-au-Bois Carency	26	-	Bn. going into line, Bn. moved two Coys. to Carency & two Coys. with Bn. Hqrs to Villers-au-Bois; Bn. in Brigade Reserve.	
"	26-30	-	Bn. remained at Carency & Villers-au-Bois, furnishing working-parties of 250 nightly in front line.	

Lt. Col.
O.C. 8th London Regt.

1875 W+. W593/826 1,000,000 4/15 J.B.C. & A. A.D.S.S./Forms/C. 2118.

XIthCorps No.G/1 (I).

SECRET.

I Corps.
IV Corps.
XI Corps.

Reference conversations on the subject with General Staff Officers for Intelligence of your Corps.

Some of the French Amplifier Sets for the purpose of tapping German telephone and telegraph messages have now arrived at G.H.Q. and are now ready for issue. It is proposed to instal one on the front of each Corps.

Kindly inform me if German speaking personnel, with a sufficient knowledge of the language, is now available.

The position for the apparatus should be chosen as soon as possible.

(Sd) W.L.O.TWISS, Major,
for Major General,
General Staff, First Army.

5/4/16.

(2)

140th Infantry Brigade.

Reference above, can you please inform me of the number of Officers or men, if any, who can understand the German language fluently.

Please treat this matter as urgent and forward numbers as soon as possible.

The apparatus when received will be located in the 47th Division front.

(Sd) H.RUTHVEN, Captain,
for General Staff,
47th (London) Division.

G/708/76.
6/4/16.

(3)

Officer Commanding
15th Bn. London Regiment.

Please forward number of Officers and men who can understand the German language fluently by 6 p.m. today without fail.

for Captain,
Brigade Major,
140th Infantry Brigade.

BRIGADE OFFICE
6 - APR. 1916
140TH INFANTRY BRIGADE

226

SCHEDULE.

UNIT.	DATE.	RELIEVED BY.	TIME.	RELIEVES.	SECTOR.	GUIDES. TIME.	PLACE.	REMARKS.
15th Bn.	April 7th.	23rd Bn.	11 a.m.	18th Bn.	Reserve.			
6th Bn.	,, 7th.	-	-	17th Bn.	Left.	1 a.m.	Sugar Factory.	
8th Bn.	,, 8th.	22nd Bn.	1 p.m.	17th Bn.	VILLERS AU BOIS.	7.45 x		
8th Bn.	,, ,,	21st Bn.	6 p.m.	20th Bn.	Right.	8.30 p.m.	CABARET ROUGE.*	
7th Bn.	,, ,,	21st Bn. ∅ ƒ	8 p.m.	15th Bn.	Reserve.			
15th Bn.	,, ,,	7th Bn.	8 p.m.	19th Bn.	Centre.	8.30 p.m.	Cross Roads X.16.c.3.3.	
140th B.M.G.Coy.	,, ,,	142nd B.M.G.Coy.	-	141st B.M.G.Coy.	Details to be arranged between O's.C. Coys.			
140/1 T.M.B.	,, ,,	142/1 T.M.B.	-	141/1 T.M.B.	Details to be arranged between O's.C. Battys.			Route as for 8th Bn.
140/2 T.M.B.	,, ,,	142/2 T.M.B.	-	141/2 T.M.B.	Details to be arranged between O's.C. Battys.			Route as for 8th Bn.

∅ Guides for 21st Bn. to be at old Brigade H.Qrs. ABLAIN ST NAZAIRE at 9 p.m.
ƒ Billeting party to be sent by this Bn. on morning of 8th instant to CARENCY and VILLERS AU BOIS.
* Route from VILLERS AU BOIS via ST.ELOI ROAD, DUCK WALK and BOYAU de REDOUBTE to CABARET ROUGE.

140th Infantry Brigade Order No.71.

(Ref.Sheets 36b and c, 1/40,000).

6th April, 1916.

1. The 140th Infantry Brigade will relieve the 141st Infantry Brigade in the line, in accordance with attached Schedule, on the 7th and 8th April, 1916.

2. Receipts will be given for all trench stores, and copies sent to this Office by 9 a.m. on the 9th instant.

3. Brigade Headquarters close at GOUY at 4 p.m. on the 8th April and reopen on arrival at VILLERS AU BOIS.

R.P.Foster Captain,
Brigade Major,
140th Infantry Brigade.

Issued at 4 pm

Copy No.		
1	Operation Order File.	
2	War Diary.	
3	47th Division.	By Signals.
4	6th Bn.Lon.Regt.	,,
5	7th ,,	,,
6	8th ,,	,,
7	15th ,,	,,
8	140 M.G.Company.	,,
9	140/1 T.M.B.	,,
10	140/2 T.M.B.	,,
11	3rd Field Coy.R.E.	,,
12	2/3rd Field Coy.R.E.	,,
13	4th Field Coy.R.E.	,,
14	141st Inf.Bde.	,,
15	142nd ,,	,,
16	Signals	,,
17	Spare	,,
18	,,	,,

238

"A" Form.   Army Form C. 2121.
MESSAGES AND SIGNALS.   No. of Message

Prefix	Code	m.	Words	Charge	This message is on a/c of:	Recd. at ... m.
Office of Origin and Service Instructions.						Date
		Sent At ... m.			Service.	From
		To				
		By			(Signature of "Franking Officer.")	By

TO   COPPER

| Sender's Number. | Day of Month | In reply to Number | AAA |

... handwritten message...

From   1/4 INF BDE
Place
Time   2.45

239

SECRET.   Copy No. 6

140th INFANTRY BRIGADE ORDER NO. 72.

Reference :- Sheets 36.B. and C.
              1-40,000.   12th April, 1916.

1.   The 140th Infantry Brigade will be relieved by the 142nd Infantry Brigade in the Line in accordance with attached schedule on 13th and 14th April, 1916.

2.   Receipts will be taken for all Trench Stores handed over, and copies sent to Brigade Headquarters by 9 a.m. on 16th April, 1916.

3.   Brigade Headquarters close at VILLERS AU BOIS at 5.30 p.m. on 14th April, 1916 and will reopen at FRESNICOURT on arrival there.

                                R V Foster Captain,
                                            Brigade Major,
                                            140th Infantry Brigade.

Copy No. 1. War Diary.   Copy No. 11. B.A.R.O.
         2. File.   12. No.4 Sect. Sigs.
         3. 47th Divn.   13. 2/3 Fd.Co.R.E.
         4. 6th Bn. Lon. Reg.   14. 141st Inf.Bde.
         5. 7th   do   15. 142nd   do
         6. 8th   do   16. Bde. T/port.Offr.
         7. 15th   do   17. Spare.
         8. 140 B.M.G.Coy.   18.   "
         9. 140/1 T.M.B.   19.   "
        10. 140/2 T.M.B.

SCHEDULE.

DATE.	UNIT.	SUB-SECTION.	RELIEVED BY.	GUIDES. TIME	GUIDES. PLACE	NEW BILLETING AREA.	REMARKS.
April 13th.	7th Battn.	Reserve.	22nd Battn.	-	-	ESTREE CAUCHIE.	Relieved at 1 p.m.
,, ,,	6th ,,	Left.	22nd ,,	9 p.m.	Road Junction S.7.d.8.2	VILLERS AU BOIS	
,, 14th	6th ,,	-	-	-	-	FRESNICOURT	Relieved at 4 p.m.
,, ,,	15th ,,	Centre.	24th ,,	8.30 p.m	Road Junction X.18.c.3.3	MAISNIL BOUCHE.	
,, ,,	8th ,,	Right.	21st ,,	8.0 pm.	CABARET ROUGE	VERDREL	

140/1 and 140/2 T.M.B's will be relieved under arrangements to be made direct with 141/1 and 141/2 T.M.B's.

NORTON.

NUMBER.	SITUATION AND OWNER.	LIME-DRESS-INGS.	CULTIVATED BY	SUB-SOIL.	UNIT.	DATE.
Levelled C.1 p.25.	GWYCHR, WALTERS POIR A.T.F.T.8.	Bond junction A.T.F.T.8.	steam plan	Peas	4th	April 18th
Levelled C.1 p.32.	ARRENICOURT.		"	clay	"	"
	WARSHIP HOUSES.	Bond junction A.T.F.T.8.	8.30 p.m	31st	clay	18th
	ENCORE.	TREVARES	6 p.m and	"	Chalk.	18th "

All referees under circumstances to be made direct with T.P.
167/3 and 191/3 T.F.F.T.8. and 190/1 and 191/1

241

SECRET.   COPY No. 6

140TH INFANTRY BRIGADE ORDER NO. 73.

Reference :- Sheets 36.B.& C. 1-40,000.

                                                    18th April, 1916.

1. The 140th Infantry Brigade will relieve the 141st Infantry Brigade in support in accordance with the attached schedule on 19th and 20th April, 1916.

2. The Officer Commanding 8th Bn. London Regt. will give a receipt for all stores taken over in LORETTE Trenches, and send a copy to Brigade Headquarters by 6 p.m. on the 21st April, 1916.

3. 140/1 and 140/2 Trench Mortar Batteries will remain at GOUY SERVINS.

4. Brigade Headquarters close at FRESNICOURT at 3.30 p.m. on 20th April, 1916 and will re-open on arrival at GOUY SERVINS.

                                            R.V.Foster Captain,
                                                    Brigade Major,
                                                    140th Infantry Brigade.

Copy No. 1. War Diary.
        2. File.
        3. 47th Divn.   By Signal Service.
        4. 6th Bn. London Regt.   ,,
        5. 7th   do.   ,,
        6. 8th   do.   ,,
        7. 15th   do.   ,,
        8. 140th B.M.G.Coy.   ,,
        9. 140/1 T.M.B.   ,,
       10. 140/2 T.M.B.   ,,
       11. Bde.Ammn.Res. Officer.   ,,
       12. Bde.Transport Officer.   ,,
       13. No. 4 Sect. Signals.   ,,
       14. 2/3rd Field Coy.R.E.   ,,
       15. 141st Inf.Bde.   ,,
       16. 142nd Inf.Bde.   ,,
       17. Spare.
       18.   ,,
       19.   ,,
       20.   ,,

140TH INFANTRY BRIGADE ORDER NO. 77.

Reference :- Sheets 36.N.W. & 57. 1:40,000.

15th April, 1916.

1. The 140th Infantry Brigade will relieve the 141st Infantry Brigade in support in accordance with the attached schedule on 15th and 20th April, 1916.

2. The Officers Commanding Btn. London Regt. will give a receipt for all stores taken over by A/141st Brigade, hand send a copy to Brigade Headquarters by 6 p.m. on 21st April, 1916.

3. 140/1 and 140/2 Trench Mortar Batteries will remain at BOUY SERVINS.

4. Brigade Headquarters close at FREMICOURT at 2.30 p.m. on 20th April, 1916 and will re-open upon arrival at BOUY SERVINS.

W.R.N. Clarke, Captain,
Brigade Major,
140th Infantry Brigade.

Copy No. 1. War Diary.
" 2. File.
" 3. 47th Divn. } by Signal Service.
" 4. 6th Bn. London Regt.
" 5. 7th do.
" 6. 8th do.
" 7. 15th do.
" 8. 140th A. & S. Coy.
" 9. 140/1 T.M.B.
" 10. 140/2 T.M.B.
" 11. Bde. Amm. Res. Officer.
" 12. Bde. Transport Officer.
" 13. No. 4 Sect. Div. Sig.
" 14. 2/4th Field Coy. R.E.
" 15. 141st Inf. Bde.
" 16. 142nd Inf. Bde.
" 17. Spare.
" 18. "
" 19. "
" 20. "

SCHEDULE.

Unit.	Unit relieved.	Date.	Time of arrival in new area.	New BILLETING Area.
8th Bn.	19th Bn.	19th April.	11 a.m.	BOUVIGNY HUTS.
8th Bn.	20th Bn.	20th ,,	-	LORETTE Trenches.
6th Bn.	8th Bn.	20th ,,	6 p.m.	BOUVIGNY HUTS.
7th Bn.	18th Bn.	20th ,,	1 p.m.	GOUY SERVINS.
15th Bn.	17th Bn.	20th ,,	6 p.m.	VILLERS AU BOIS.

NOTE. Guides for LORETTE Trenches will meet 8th Bn. at old Brigade Headquarters ABLAIN ST NAZAIRE 8.30 p.m.

"A" Form.   Army Form C. 2121.

MESSAGES AND SIGNALS.   No. of Message _____

Office of Origin and Service Instructions. Code AAA	Words 7	Charge	This message is on a/c of: ....Service. (Signature of "Franking Officer.")	Recd. at ...... m. Date ...... From ...... By ......
Sent At ...... m. To ...... By ......

TO { 6th LON REGT

| Sender's Number 3/MG/78 | Day of Month 26 | In reply to Number | AAA |

Please arrange to have two sections of your grenadiers detailed with your companies tonight.

From 140 INFANTRY BRIGADE 10 pm
Place
Time

244

SECRET.   Copy No...... 6

140TH INFANTRY BRIGADE ORDER NO.74.

Reference :-
   Sheets 38.b.& c.
   1/40,000.

                                              24th April, 1916.

1.   The 140th Infantry Brigade will relieve the 141st Infantry Brigade in the line in accordance with attached Schedule on 25/26th April, 1916.

2.   Receipts will be given for all Trench stores and copies sent to this office by 9 a.m. on 27th April.

3.   Brigade Headquarters close at GOUY at 4 p.m. on the 26th April, and re-open on arrival at VILLERS AU BOIS.

                                                Captain,
                                                Brigade Major,
                                                140th Infantry Brigade.

Copy No.1. War Diary.
       2. File.
       3. 47th Division.   By Signal Sect.
       4. 6th Bn. London Regt.   ,,
       5. 7th   do.   ,,
       6. 8th   do.   ,,
       7.15th   do.   ,,
       8. B.M.G.Coy.   ,,
       9. 140/1 T.M.B.   ,,
     10. 140/2 T.M.B.   ,,
     11. Bde.Amm.Res.Officer.   ,,
     12. Bde.Transport Officer. ,,
     13. Bde.Bomb.Officer.   ,,
     14. No.4 Sect.Signals.   ,,
     15. 2/3rd Coy.R.E.   ,,
     16. 141st Inf. Bde.   ,,
     17. 142nd Inf. Bde.   ,,
     18. Spare.
     19. ,,
     20. ,,

SCHEDULE.

Date.	Unit.	Relieved by.	Relieves	Sector.	Guides. Place.	Guides. Time.	Remarks.
April 25	6th Bn	22nd Bn (at 11am)	20th Bn (at 1pm)	RESERVE. (VILLERS AU BOIS & CARENCY)	-	-	-
,, 25	15th Bn	-	17th Bn	LEFT	Sugar Factory ABLAIN	9 pm	-
,, 26	7th Bn	24th Bn (at 1pm)	17th Bn (at 2pm)	VILLERS AU BOIS	-	-	-
,, 26	6th Bn	8th Bn	19th Bn	CENTRE	X.16.c.3.3	8.30 pm	-
,, 26	8th Bn	22nd Bn	6th Bn	RESERVE (Old Brigade H.Q.) (VILLERS AU BOIS & CARENCY)	ABLAIN	8 pm	Guides for 22nd Bn. to be supplied by 8th Bn.
,, 26	7th Bn	21st Bn (at 6 pm)	18th Bn	RIGHT	CABARET ROUGE	8.30 pm	Route from VILLERS AU BOIS via ST.ELOI, DUCKWALK & BOYAU de REDOUBTE to CABARET ROUGE.
,, 26	140/1 T.M.B.	142/1 T.M.B.	141/1 T.M.B.	Details to be arranged between O's C. Batteries.			
,, 26	140/2 T.M.B.	142/2 T.M.B.	141/2 T.M.B.	Details to be arranged between O's C. Batteries.			

246

Copy No. 11

8th London Regiment
(Post Office Rifles)

Operation Order No. 6, by Captain W.B. Vince.
8th ~~March~~ April 1916.

Reference. — Map 36 B, 3rd edition, 1/40,000.

① The Bn. will relieve the 20th London Regt: in the Right Sub-section, CARENCY sector to-night.

② Guides of the 20th Bn. will be at Cabaret Rouge at 7.45 p.m.

③ The Bn. will leave VILLERS in the following order — Bombers, No. 3 Coy (Left), No. 2 Coy (Centre), No. 4 Coy (Right), No. 1 Coy (Support), Bn. Hqrs. — starting at 5.30 p.m., with an interval of 100 yards between platoons and two minutes between Coys.

Route — ST. ELOI ROAD — DUCK WALK — BOYAU DE LA REDOUTE.

④ Coys: and detachments will give receipts for trench stores, & will send copies of them to Bn. Hqrs. within an hour of completion of relief.

⑤ Rations will be issued after completion of relief.

⑥ Bn. Hqrs. & Dressing Station — S 14 b 70, 85.

Steel
Capt: & Adjt:
8th London Regt:
(Post Office Rifles)

Issued at 9 a.m.
Copy No. 1 — File
" " 2 — 140th Infy. Bde.
" " 3 — No. 1 Coy
" " 4 — 2 "
" " 5 — 3 "
" " 6 — 4 "
" " 7 — Lewis Gun Officer
" " 8 — ~~Lewis~~ Bombing Officer
" " 9 — Quartermaster
" " 10 — Transport Officer
" " 11 — War Diary.

247

Copy No. 12

References:-
France, sheets 36B
3rd Edt. 1/40,000

8th London Regt. (Post Office Rifles)

Operation Order No 8
by Lt. Col. L. Maxwell

20th April 1916

(1) The Bn. will relieve the 20th London Regt. in the LORETTE TRENCHES to-night.

(2) Coys will pass Bn. Hqrs. as follows and proceed by the route reconnoitred last night, meeting their guides at 8-30 in the same place as last night, i.e. Old Brigade Hqrs. AB4A/N.
   No. 4 Coy - 7-30 p.m.   No. 3 Coy: 7-33   Bombers 7-36
   No. 1 Coy - 7-30   No. 2 Coy - 7-40

½ No. 2 Coy. will be detached en route and proceed under separate orders issued to 2 Lt. Smith.

(3) The Lewis Gun Detachment will move with its limbers at 7-15 and proceed via GOUY and the ABLAIN road, meeting its guides at the same place as the Coys.

(4) Receipts will be given for all stores taken over, and copies sent to Orderly Room by 9 a.m. to-morrow.

(5) Bn. Hqrs: X 10 & 41

(6) Rations and water will be drawn after the Bn. has been taken over, parties being sent by Nos 1, 3 & 4 Coys, Bombers, & Lewis Gun Detachment to the dump at the SUCRERIE at 11-30 p.m., by ½ No. 2 Coy: to B. Hq. at 11-30 p.m., & by ½ No. 2 Coy: under 2 Lt. Smith to R. 33 C. at 6 a.m.

(7) The 6th Bn. will arrive to take over BOUVIGNY HUTS at 6 p.m. Huts will be ready for handing over at that time, & all equipment etc ready for move, but Coys: will not move across or vacate huts until orders to move out.

(8) Hqr. limber will move off with Lewis Gun Detachment. Coy. boxes to reach Bn. Hqrs. not later than 6-30. Two servants per Coy. will march with the limber.

Copy No. 1 - File
   2 - 140th Infantry Brigade
   3 - 141st
   4 - OC. No. 1 Coy
   5 -   "   " 2 "
   6 -   "   " 3 "
   7 -   "   " 4 "
   8 - Lewis Gun Officer
   9 - Bombing   "
   10 - Quartermaster
   11 - Transport Officer
   12 - War Diary

Neel
Capt. & Adjt.
8th London Regt.
(P.O.R.)

8th London Regt (Post Office Rifles)

Operation Order No 8
by Lt Col A Maxwell

20th April 1916

Reference:
France, Sheet 36B
3rd Edt 1/20000.

(1) The Bn will relieve the 6th Bn Suss Regt in the LORETTE TRENCHES tonight.

(2) Coys will leave Bns Hqrs as follows and proceed by the road mentioned last night, making their guides at the same place as last night, i.e. the Brigade Sign 18.a.4.N.
    No 4 Coy - 7.30 p.m.   No 3 Coy - 7.33   Bombers 7.3[?]
    No 1 Coy - 7.30   No 2 Coy - 7.3[?]

    No 2 Coy will be detached en route and proceed under separate orders [?] to 2 Lt Smith.

(3) The Lewis Gun Detachment will move with HQ Section at 7.15 and proceed via JOUY and the ABLAIN road, meeting its guides at the same place as the Coys.

(4) Receipts will be given for all stores taken over, and copies sent to Orderly Room by 9 a.m. to morrow.

(5) Bn Hqrs: X.10.b.41

(6) Rations and water will be drawn after the Bn has been taken over, parties being sent by Nos 1, 3 & 4 Coys, Bombers, & Lewis Gun Detachment to be dump at the SUCRERIE at 4.30 a.m., by No 4 Coy at 4.[?]0 at 4.30 a.m., & by No 2 Coy in its own billets. Rations [?]

(7) The 6th Bn will arrive to take over BOUVIGNY HUTS at 6 p.m. Huts will be ready for handing over at that time, & all equipment be ready for move, but Coys will not leave huts or vacate huts until ordered to
move [?] out.

(8) Aqr. Limbers will move off with Lewis Gun Detachment. Coy. boxes to reach Bn Hqrs not later than 6-30. Two servants per Coy. will march with the Limbers.

Copies - File
1 - 140th Infantry Brigade
3 - 141st "
4 - OC No 1 Coy
5 - "   " 2 "
6 - "   " 3 "
7 - "   " 4 "
8 - Lewis Gun Officer
9 - Bombing "
10 - Quartermaster
11 - Transport Officer
12 - War Diary

Neil
Capt & Adjt
8th London Regt
P.O.R.

262

8th Batt⁹. London Reg⁹.

Operation Order No. 9   30-4-16.

1) The Batt⁹. will be relieved by 23rd Bn. at 1p.m. to-morrow.
2) Coys & detachments will move off independently as soon as relieved & will proceed to ESTREE CAUCHIE.
3) Certificates of cleanliness will be taken from relieving Bn.
4) Blankets & valises will be stacked at Bn. HQRS by 10 a.m.
5) Cookers, & water cart & medical cart will move off independently after breakfast.
6) Hdqr limber will leave HQRS at 10.30 a.m. Coy boxes to reach HQRS by 10.15 a.m.
7) Lewis Gun limber will move with the 2 L.G. sections.
8) Dinners on arrival at ESTREE CAUCHIE.
9) Rouse 8, Breakfast 9, Sick 10.

                       (sgd) H. Peel.
                           (Capt & Adjt).
                     8th London Regt.

263

SECRET.

47th (LONDON) DIVISION.

PROGRAMME OF INFANTRY RELIEFS FOR MAY 1916.

TRENCH BRIGADE	DATE	SUPPORT BRIGADE
142 Bde relieves 140 Bde	May 2nd	141 Bde relieves 142 Bde
141 ,, ,, 142 ,,	May 8th	140 ,, ,, 141 ,,
140 ,, ,, 141 ,,	May 14th	142 ,, ,, 140 ,,
142 ,, ,, 140 ,,	May 20th	141 ,, ,, 142 ,,
141 ,, ,, 142 ,,	May 26th	140 ,, ,, 141 ,,
140 ,, ,, 141 ,,	June 1st	142 ,, ,, 140 ,,

NOTES (i) Command of Support Brigade will be handed over at 3.30 p.m. and Command of Trench Brigade at 5.30 p.m. on day of relief.

(ii) Left Subsection will be relieved on night previous to, and Right and Centre Subsections on night after, Brigade Headquarters move.

(iii) All movements will be carried out in accordance with programme laid down in G/863/26 dated 17/3/16. Details to be arranged direct between G.Os.C. Brigades.

General Staff,
47th (London) Division.

G/863/26/1.

27th April 1916.

SECRET.   COPY No........

140TH INFANTRY BRIGADE ORDER No.75.

Reference :-
  Sheets 36 b. & c.
  1/40,000.   30th April, 1916.

1. The 140th Infantry Brigade will be relieved in the line by the 142nd Infantry Brigade in accordance with accompanying schedule on 1/2nd May, 1916.

2. Receipts will be taken for all Trench Stores and copies sent to this office by 9 a.m. 3rd May.

3. Brigade Headquarters close at VILLERS AU BOIS at 5.30 p.m. 2nd May, and reopen on arrival at FRESNICOURT.

                                            R.V.Foster
                                                Captain,
                                              Brigade Major,
                                            140th Infantry Brigade.

Copy No. 1. War Diary.
         2. File.
         3. 47th Divn.   By Signal Service.
         4. 6th Bn. London Regt.   ,,
         5. 7th   do.   ,,
         6. 8th   do.   ,,
         7. 15th   do.   ,,
         8. B.M.G.Coy.   ,,
         9. Bde.Amm.Res.Officer.   ,,
        10. Bde.Bomb Officer.   ,,
        11. Bde.Transport Officer.   ,,
        12. No. 4 Sig.Section.   ,,
        13. 140/1 T.M.B.   ,,
        14. 140/2 T.M.B.   ,,
        15. 2/3rd Fd.Coy.R.E.   ,,
        16. 141st Inf. Bde.   ,,
        17. 142nd Inf. Bde.   ,,
        18. Spare.
        19.   ,,
        20.   ,,

SCHEDULE.

DATE.	UNIT.	SECTION.	RELIEVED BY	GUIDES.		BILLETING AREA.
				PLACE.	TIME.	
May 1st.	8th Bn.	RESERVE.	23rd Bn. (1 p.m.)			ESTREE CAUCHIE.
May 1st.	15th Bn.	LEFT.	23rd Bn.	SUGAR FACTORY.	9 p.m.	VILLERS AU BOIS.
May 2nd.	15th Bn.		24th Bn. (2 p.m.)			FRESNICOURT.
May 2nd.	8th Bn.	CENTRE.	24th Bn.	CABARET ROUGE.	8.30 p.m.	VERDREL.
*May 2nd.	7th Bn.	RIGHT.	21st Bn.	CABARET ROUGE.	8.30 p.m.	MAISNIL BOUCHE.

" 140/1 and 140/2 T.M.B's. will be relieved by 142/1 and 142/2 T.M.B's. under arrangements to be made by O's.C. Batteries.

* Reliefs in and out for RIGHT Sector will move via VILLERS AU BOIS, DUCK WALK and CABARET ROUGE Road to CABARET ROUGE.

SECRET.   COPY No........

140TH INFANTRY BRIGADE ORDER No.76.

Reference :- Sheets 36 b & c.   In the Field.
              1/40,000.   6th May, 1916.

1.   The 140th Inf. Bde. will relieve the 141st Inf. Bde. in Support on May 7th and 8th.

2.   All moves will be in accordance with accompanying schedule.

3.   Receipts will be taken for Trench stores in LORETTE Trenches, and copy of receipt forwarded to this office by 6 p.m. May 9th.

4.   Brigade Headquarters will close at FRESNICOURT at 3 p.m. 8th May, and will reopen on arrival at GOUY.

                                     Captain,
                               Brigade Major,
                          140th Infantry Brigade.

Copy No.1. War Diary.
      2. File.
      3. 47th Divn.   By Signal Service.
      4. 6th Bn.   do.
      5. 7th Bn.   do.
      6. 8th Bn.   do.
      7.15th Bn.   do.
      8. B.M.G.Coy.   do.
      9. 140/1 T.M.B.   do.
    10. 140/2 T.M.B.   do.
    11. Bde.Bomb.Offr.   do.
    12. Bde.Transport Offr.   do.
    13. No.4 Sect.Signals.
    14. Bde.Amm.Res.Offr.   do.
    15. 2/3rd Fd.Co.R.E.   do.
    16. 141st Inf. Bde.   do.
    17. 142nd Inf. Bde.   do.
    18. Spare.
    19.   ,,
    20.   ,,

SCHEDULE.

DATE.	UNIT.	UNIT RELIEVED.	TIME.	New BILLETING area.
May 7th.	6th Bn.	18th Bn.	11. a.m.	BOUVIGNY HUTS.
May 8th.	8th Bn.	20th Bn.	1 p.m.	GOUY SERVINS.
" "	15th Bn.	6th Bn.	8 p.m.	BOUVIGNY HUTS.
" "	7th Bn.	20th Bn.	6 p.m.	VILLERS AU BOIS.
" "	* 6th Bn.	19th Bn.	-	LORETTE TRENCHES.

* Guides for 6th Bn. will be at old Bde. Hdqrs. ABLAIN, at 8.30 p.m.

War Diary   Copy No 11

Operation Order No 10.   Long Service
by Lt. Col. A. Maxwell.   10th May 1916.

(1) The Bn. will relieve the 11th Lancashire Fusiliers in the
    Left Sub-Section, "B" (Beaumont) Sector to-morrow
    night.

(2) Guides of the 11th Lancashire Fusiliers will be at Cabaret
    Rouge at 9.30 p.m.

(3) The Bn. will parade in column of route, head of the
    column at the outer gate of the chateau ready to
    move off at 5.55 p.m., and will move with a two-minute
    interval between coys. to Villers au Bois where there will
    be a halt for about an hour. Order of march Hqrs., 1, 2
    3, 4. Bombers, Lewis Gun Detachment.
    Coy gear, Coy Signallers, Stretcher Bearers, & Bn. Orderlies with their
    coys.

(4) Coys & Detachments will proceed to the trenches in the following
    order: No. 1 Coy with 1 section of Bombers, No. 4 Coy, No. 2 Coy, No. 3 Coy
    Hqrs. with remainder of Bombers, Lewis Gun. They will move
    from Villers till ordered. Route via Cabaret Road
    & Ersatz alley except for Lewis Gun Detachment, for which
    separate orders will be issued.

(5) Rations will be distributed after the completion of relief.
    Full water-bottles will be carried.

(6) Copies of receipts given for Trench Stores will be sent to Bn.
    Hqrs. as soon as possible after completion of relief.

                                                    HWL
                                                Capt. & Adjt.
                                            8th Bn. London Regt.
                                              (Post Office Rifles)

Nos. 1 Coy.
 " 2 " (and Lewis Gun Off.)
 " 3 " Coy
 " 4 "
 " 5 "
 " 6 "
 " 7 Lewis Gun Officer
 " 8 Bombing Officer
 " 9 Scouts
 " 10 Transport Officer
 " 11 War Diary
 " 12 Hqrs.

269

SECRET.

Copy No...... 6

140th INFANTRY BRIGADE ORDER NO.80.

(Ref. FRANCE, LENS 1i, 1/100000).

24th May, 1916.

1. The Brigade will move tomorrow in accordance with March Table.

2. Machine Guns and teams now in action will remain in line under orders of G.O.C., 99th Infantry Brigade.

3. Billeting parties of 1 Officer, 1 N.C.O. and 5 other ranks mounted or on cycles will meet Staff Captain as follows:-
BRUAY	Town Major's Office	8.0 a.m.
CALONNE RICOUART	Station.	11.0 a.m.
CAMBLAIN CHATELAIN	Church	11.30 a.m.

4. Attention is drawn to Divisional Standing Orders (War), paras. 36 and 38 which must be strictly complied with. All Officers and N.C.O's must be acquainted with Section III of above and also with paras. 21-27 of 4th London Infantry Brigade Standing Orders for War.

5. Transport will be Brigaded under the Brigade Transport Officer and will follow Machine Gun Company in order of march of Units.

6. Brigade Headquarters will close at CHATEAN d'ACQ at 6.45 a.m. and will reopen on arrival at BRUAY.

                                                          Major,
Brigade Major,
140th Infantry Brigade.

Copy No. 1   File.
,,   2   War Diary.
,,   3   47th Division.
,,   4   6th Bn. Lon. Regt.
,,   5   7th ,,
,,   6   8th ,,
,,   7   15th ,,
,,   8   140 B.M.G.Coy.
        (Cabaret Rouge)
,,   9   140 B.M.G.Coy.
        (Camblain l'Abbé)
,,   10   No.2 Coy. 47th Div. Train.
,,   11   Staff Captain.
,,   12   140/1 and 140/2 T.M.B's.
,,   13   Brigade Transport Officer.
,,   14   No.4 Section, 47th Div. Sigs.
,,   15   Brigade Amm. Reserve Offr.
,,   16   Brigade Bombing Officer.
,,   17   99th Infantry Brigade.
,,   18   Spare.
,,   19   ,,
,,   20   ,,

MARCH TABLE.

UNIT.	Disposal.	Time of passing Starting point.	Billeting Area.	Remarks.
Brigade Headquarters	--	a.m. 8.0	BRUAY.	
8th Battalion	Leading Battalion	8.1	CAMBLAIN CHATELAIN	
15th "	Battalion at disposal	8.4	CALONNE RICOUART	
5th "	Battalion on duty	8.8	BRUAY	
7th "	Rear Battalion	8.12	BRUAY	
Machine Gun Coy. (less Transport for guns in action)	--	8.15	BRUAY	
Transport	--	8.18	--	

STARTING POINT:- Point 150 S.E. of LES QUATRE VENTS on the ESTREE CAUCHIE - ARRAS Road.

SECRET.   Copy No...

140TH INFANTRY BRIGADE.

OPERATION ORDER No.77.

Reference:- Sheets 36 b & c.
1/40,000.   In the field.
                             10th May, 1916.

1.   The 15th Bn.London Regt. will relieve the 6th Bn.London Regt. in the LORETTE Trenches on the evening of Sunday next, 14th May, under arrangements to be made direct by the Commanding Officers concerned.
    After being relieved the 6th Battalion will move to BOUVIGNY HUTS.
2.   Copies of Battalion Operation Orders to be forwarded to this office 24 hours previous to the relief.
3.   A copy of the receipt for Trench stores will be forwarded to this office by 6.0 p.m. 15th May.
4.   Completion of relief to be reported to this office.

                                                  Captain,
                                          Acting Brigade Major,
                                        140th Infantry Brigade.

Copy No. 1. War Diary.
       2. File.
       3. 47th Divn.   By Signal Service.
       4. 47th Divn.C.R.E.   ,,
       5. 6th Bn.London Regt.   ,,
       6. 7th   do.   ,,
       7. 8th   do.   ,,
       8. 15th   do.   ,,
       9. Bde.M.G.Coy.   ,,
      10. 140/1 T.M.B.   ,,
      11. 140/2 T.M.B.   ,,
      12. Bde.Bombing Offr.   ,,
      13. Bde.Amm.Res.Offr.   ,,
      14. Bde.Transport Offr.   ,,
      15. No.4 Sig.Coy.   ,,
      16. 1/3rd Fd.Coy.R.E.   ,,
      17. 141st.Inf.Bde.   ,,
      18. 142nd.Inf.Bde.   ,,
      19. Spare.
      20. ,,

SECRET.

Officer Commanding,
~~6th Bn. London Regt.~~   140 ~~B.M.G. Coy.~~
~~7th Bn. London Regt.~~   140 ~~D.M. Battery.~~
8th Bn. London Regt.   2nd ~~H.M.Bn.~~
~~15th Bn. London Regt.~~

A Series of Minor Operations will shortly be carried out on the front of the 47th Division and adjoining Division, with a view to harassing the enemy and holding him to his ground.

Wire cutting will be carried out by the Divisional Artillery and Medium Trench Mortars under the orders of the C.R.A. on portions of the whole of the Divisional front.

Officers Commanding Battalions holding the line will arrange to keep any gaps made in the enemy's wire under fire of Machine or Lewis Guns and rifles during the hours of darkness and so preventing the enemy repairing his wire.

B.M.898.
22/6/16.

Major,
Brigade Major,
140th Infantry Brigade.

227

140th Brigade.
47th Division.

1/8th BATTALION

LONDON REGIMENT

JULY 1916

Army Form C. 2118.

1/8th Battr.
London Regt.

Vol 17

WAR DIARY
or
INTELLIGENCE SUMMARY.
(Erase heading not required.)

Place	Date	Hour	Summary of Events and Information	Remarks and references to Appendices
	July 1		Bn. in Souchez II Sector. One coy. of Drake Bn. R.N.D. attached for instruction. Other Ranks wounded 3. Reinforcement of 148 other ranks received.	
	" 2.		Remained in Trenches. Other ranks died of wounds 1 wounded 4.	
	" 3		Remained in Trenches. 15th Bn. London Regt. in SOUCHEZ I Sector on our right carried out a raid on enemy trenches in BOIS EN HACHE.	
	" 4		Enemy shelled our right Coy. with minenwerfer. Other ranks wounded 6. Bn. was relieved by 6th Bn. London Regt. and marched to huts in BOIS DE NOULETTE. 2 Lt. Pearce transferred to 1/3rd London Regt.	
	5-6.		Batt. remained in BOIS DE NOULETTE	
	7		Bn. was relieved by 20th Batt. and moved to BOUVIGNY BOYEFFLES and took over billets of 18th Batt. London Regt. Enemy shelled village. Other ranks 1 killed 7 wounded.	
	8.		Batt. at BOUVIGNY BOYEFFLES. Major Thin 2/2nd London Regt. joined.	
	9		Ditto. Ditto.	
	10		Ditto. Ditto.	
	11		Ditto. Ditto. Enemy again shelled village. Other ranks wounded 2.	
	12		Ditto. Ditto.	

Army Form C. 2118.

WAR DIARY
or
INTELLIGENCE SUMMARY.
(Erase heading not required.)

Instructions regarding War Diaries and Intelligence Summaries are contained in F.S. Regs., Part II. and the Staff Manual respectively. Title pages will be prepared in manuscript.

Place	Date	Hour	Summary of Events and Information	Remarks and references to Appendices
	July 13		Batt. at BOUVIGNY BOYEFFLES. 2/Sgt Kramer, Rfn. E. Hands and Rfn. B. Moyne awarded Military Medals.	
	14		Batt. at BOUVIGNY BOYEFFLES.	
	15		Batt. relieved 22nd Royal Fusiliers in BERTHONVAL Sector.	
	16		Batt. in trenches. Lt Nathan and one other rank wounded.	
	17		Batt. in trenches. Enemy bombarded left and centre Coys. with minenwerfer. 10 other rank killed & one wounded	
	18		Batt. in trenches. Enemy's minenwerfer again active. 4 other ranks wounded.	
	19-20		Batt. in trenches.	
	21		Batt. was relieved by 6th Batt. and moved into support at CABARET ROUGE.	
	22-24		Batt. remained at CABARET ROUGE	
	25		Batt. was relieved by 8th L. Lincolns moved into billets at ESTRÉE CAUCHIE.	
	26		Batt. moved by march route to OURTON.	
	27		Batt. moved by march route to BRYAS.	
	28		Batt. remained at BRYAS.	
	29		Ditto. Inspection by G.O.C. 1st Army. 2/Lt Huggins transferred to 1/1st London Regt.	
	30		Batt. moved to BLANGERVAL. 2 Lt Auld back transferred to 1/1st London Regt.	
	31		Batt. remained at BLANGERVAL.	

W. J. Mitchell,
Lt. Col.
Commanding 8th Bn. London Regt.
(Post Office Rifles)

3/8/16

Operation Order   Copy No. 1
No. 16   1/7/16.
by Major W.J. Whitehead, O.C. 8th London Regt.

① The following changes will take place to-night.

One platoon, DRAKE BN. will relieve the platoon of No. 1 Coy: in the STRAIGHT

One platoon, DRAKE BN., will relieve platoon of No. 1 Coy: in HQRS. TRENCH.

One platoon, DRAKE BN., will relieve platoon of No. 1 Coy: in BAJOLLE LINE.

One platoon, DRAKE BN., will relieve two platoons of No. 4 Coy in the STRAIGHT.

Dug-out platoons will remain where they are.

② The relieved platoons will move to BOIS 6 and be under the command of O.C. No. 2 Coy.

③ One guide from each of the platoons of the 8th Bn: referred to in ① will report at Bn. Hqrs at 8-30 p.m.

④ Five guides from No. 2 Coy: will report at Bn. Hqrs. at 10 p.m.

⑤ O.C. No. 1 Coy: will remain in the line, having under him 1 platoon of his own and three platoons of the DRAKE BN.   O.C. No. 4

- 2 -

Coy. will remain in the line, having under him
1 platoon of his own and 1 platoon of the
DRAKE BN. The O.C. Coy. DRAKE BN. will
stay at No 1 Coy. Hqrs. & 2nd in command Coy.
Drake Bn will stay at No 4 Coy. Hqrs.

(6) The rations & water of the relieved platoons will
be taken direct to BOIS 6 from FRENCH
DUMP. OC No 2 Coy. will re-arrange ration
parties accordingly. The Coy. of DRAKE
BN. will bring in their own rations.

(7) Platoons when relieved will move off
independently with the guides sent to them
from Bn Hqrs., reporting to Bn Hqrs. by
number as they move off.

Issued at 5.30 p.m.

No. 1 Copy - file
  " 2   "   No. 1 Coy
  " 3   "   " 2 "
  " 4   "   " 3 "
  " 5   "   " 4 "
  " 6   "   140th Inf. Bde.

H. Peel
Capt. & Adjt.
St London Regt
I. O. R.

4/7/16

Copy No. —

Operation Order No. 17
by Major W. J. Whitehead, O.C. 8th London Regt.

(1) Bn. will be relieved by 6th Bn. to-night. Drake Coy: attached will be relieved by another Drake Coy:.

(2) Arrangements for relief of No. 2 Coy. & attached platoons will be made direct between O.C. No. 2 Coy: & O.C. D Coy of 6th Bn.

(3) Guides will report at Bn: Hqrs as follows:—
One guide from each Drake platoon at 8-30 p.m.
One platoon guide from No. 1 Coy
Two   "   "   "   " " 4 " } at 9-30 p.m.
Four   "   "   "   " " 3 "

(4) Bombers & Lewis gun relieve about 5 p.m. under arrangements already communicated to L.G.O. & B.O.

(5) Regtl. S. Major, Coy. S. Majors, Signallers, and 1 N.C.O. & 6 men of A & B Coys. of 6th Bn. will arrive about 6 p.m. Guides will be arranged from Bn: Hqrs.

(6) Order of relief:—
 (1) Drake platoon attached No. 1 Coy in STRAIGHT
 (2)   "   "   "   " 4 "
 (3)   "   "   "   " 1 "   HQRS TRENCH
 (4)   BAJOLLE
 (5) Platoon of 6th Bn. A Coy relieving No. 1 Coy.
 (6) 2 Platoons   "   C   "   "   " 4 "
 (7) 4   "   "   B   "   "   " 3 "

(7) On relief Coys: will move off independently, the Drake Coy: rejoining its Bn, the 8th Bn. marching to BOIS DE NOULETTE. Guides will meet out-going Coys. of 8th at COLONELS HOUSE.

II

(8) Dug-out platoons will not move with the Battalion but remain in the trenches & carry on as now. They will send parties to FRENCH DUMP at 10-15 to-night to meet limber bringing their rations. On succeeding nights their rations will be brought up to dump on 6th Bn carts, & they will send to dump to draw them.

(9) Rations, cookers & officers' kit will be at BOIS DE NOULETTE before Bn arrives.

(10) Code word for relief complete is
 OSWALD.

Neal
Capt & Adjt.
8th London Regt.
(P.O.R.)

Copy No. 1

Operation Order No. 7a.
by Major W. J. Whitehead, O.C. 8th London Regt.

(1) The Bn. will be relieved to-night by the 20th London Regt. and will move to BOUVIGNY-BOYEFFLES.

(2) The four Coy. Quartermaster-Sergeants, a representative each from the Bombers & Lewis Gun Detachments, and Corporal Turner to represent Hqrs. will parade at Orderly Room at 2.15 p.m. and proceed as billeting party to BOUVIGNY-BOYEFFLES where they will meet the Quartermaster.

(3) A guide for each Coy. and Detachment and A/Cpl. Johnson for Hqrs. will parade at Orderly Room at 9-15 p.m. and proceed under the Subaltern of the Day to meet the 20th Bn.

(4) Officers' kits will be stacked at the Recreation Hut by 5 p.m.

(5) Cookers, water-carts, M.O. cart will move off after teas.

(6) Coys. & Detachments will move off independently when relieved and will be met by billeting party at entrance to BOUVIGNY BOYEFFLES.

Copy No. 1 - File
" " 2 - M.I. Coy
" " 3 - " 2 "
" " 4 - " 3 "
" " 5 - " 4 "
" " 6 - Hqrs
" " 7 - Bo
" " 8 - TO
" " 9 - Qur
" " 10 - 140th Inf. Bde.
" " 11 - War Diary

A. Bell
Capt. & Adjt.
8th London Regt.
(P.W.R.)

7 July 1916

file

Operation Order No 18   Copy No 11
by Major W. J. Whitehead
O C 8th Battalion London Regt.
        (P. O. R)   15 July 916

1. The 8th Battn will relieve 1. 22nd 27 in the Berthonval Sector today.

2. Guides will meet Coys at Cabaret Rouge at 11-15pm. L.G.O. + B.O. will arrange Guides independently.

3. Officers detailed to reconnoitre trenches will leave at 5pm

4. Coys will move off as follows.
            1   Bombers   5.30
            2. No 4 Coy   5.35 pm
            3. " 2   5.40
            4. " 1   5.45
            5. " 3   5.50
            6   H Qrs   5.55

    The R.S.M and signallers will move off at 3 p.m. Coys will march via BOUVIGNY HUTS to VILLERS-AU-BOIS; a halt will be made in the field at the junction of the GRAND SERVINS + CARENCY ROADS, where 24 hour rations will be issued + carried into the trenches
    Lewis Gun Section + Limber will move off at 5-15 pm - proceed to CARENCY via BOUVIGNY HILL, GOUY SERVINS, VILLERS STATION SUNK ROAD

5. Nos 1 + 2 Coy Cookers and 1 water cart will leave at 3pm + proceed to VILLERS-AU-BOIS where teas will be served. Nos 3 + 4 Cookers will leave at 5-30pm with G. S. Waggon, 1 water cart + M.O. cart + proceed direct to Q.M. Stores at GRAND SERVINS.

6. Officers valises will be stacked at Chateau by 3 p.m.

7. H Qrs limber will be at Chateau at 5 am. no mess boxes will be carried

O's C Coys may each send 2 servants with not more than 2 Sandbags each. These servants with HQ servants will move off under A/Cpl Moxey at 5.30 pm.

8. The following officers will go into the trenches with the Battn

No 1	No 2	No 3	No 4
2/Lt J B Mitchell	Lt H.L Nathan	2/Lt H.O. Webb	Capt. A. S. Thomas.
J.W Deverell	2/Lt O.S.C. Chichester	" B. Watson	2/Lt E. B. Davies
A.A. Auerbach	2.J. Rew	H.R. Marsden	C.S.B. Cook
C.E. Willows	H.M Flower		J.R. Rodgers.
	L.G.O. 2/Lt M.C. Starling		
	B.O. P.E Coote }		
	R.M. Kelly }		

2/Lts. Appleton & Huggins will move to GRAND SERVINS this afternoon.
Q. M. will arrange billets

9. Relief complete to be reported at once to Battn H.Q.rs code word
RUTHYEN.

                         A Monsburgh
                         2/Lt & a/adjt.
                         8th London Regt
                         P.O.R

Copy No 1   to File
       2   140th Infy Brigade
       3   O.C No 1 Coy
       4   "   2
       5   "   3
       6   "   4
       7   L.G.O
       8   B.O.
       9   Transit Officer
      10   Q.M.
      11   War Diary

                                              Issued at 12-45 pm

279

Operation Order No 19   Copy No 3
by Major W. J. Whitehead.
Commanding 8th Bn London Regt (P.O.R.)

21st July 1916

1) The Battn will be relieved by 6th Bn London Regt in BERTHONVAL II on night of 21st-22nd July 1916 and move into Support at CABARET ROUGE

2) One Officer and NCO per Coy and the R.S.M. will reconnoitre the line to-morrow reporting at Orderly Room at 10 am

3) Guides will be detailed as follows

    Lewis Gun Detchmt   5 p.m.   at 6th Bn H.Q.R.S.
    No 1 Coy   9.45 p.m.   ditto
    " 3 "   9.45 p.m.   ditto
    " 2 "   9.30 p.m.   At junction of DUCKS WALK and COLISEUM TRENCH
    " 4 "   10 p.m.   HQRS of "D" Coy. 6th Bn in ZOUAVE VALLEY

Bombers will be relieved with their Coys.,
Signallers at 8.30 p.m.

4) O.C. No 1 Coy will detail 3 N.C.O's and 9 men to relieve Control Posts at CABARET ROUGE. They will report at Orderly Room under 2nd Lt Deverell at 4 p.m.

5) O.C. Coys will report relief complete, code word "BUNGO". On completion of relief Coys will move independently to their new positions in SUPPORT.

6) All trench Stores with the exception of periscopes will be handed over and receipts obtained. These should be forwarded to Orderly Room by 9 a.m. on 22nd inst.

A W Horsburgh
2nd Lt & a/Adjt.
8th Bn London Regt
(Post Office Rifles)

Copy No 1 To File
" " 2 " 140th Inf Bde
" " 3 " WAR DIARY.

Bombers   Rnk |||| WR   1 J.B.M.   3 T.B.W.
                                2   4

280

Copy No 6

Operation Order No 20.
by Lt Col W.J. Whitehead
Commanding 8th Bn London Regt (P.O.R)
25th July 1916

Ref. FRANCE 36B 1/40,000.

1) The Bn will be relieved by 8th LINCOLNS to-night and will move into billets at ESTREE CAUCHIE.

2) Guides. The following will parade at O.R. at 11 p.m. to-night
 2/Lt Jacob and 4 guides per Coy.
 4 guides from Bombing Platoon
 1 guide from Bn HQRS.

These guides will meet incoming Bn at junction of WORTLEY AVENUE and BOYAU 123 at 12 midnight

Guides from Lewis Gun Detachment will meet incoming Detachment at Bn HQRS at 10 p.m.

3) Move. On relief Coys and Detachments will move independently to ESTREE via Transport Track, VILLERS-AU-BOIS, MAISNIL BOUCHE.

4) Reports. O.C. Coys and detachments will report relief complete to Bn HQRS before

Code word "WERWA"

5) Limbers. Lewis Gun limber will be at CABARET ROUGE at 11 pm and will move off with L.G. Detachment.
Other limber for Headquarters will be at CABARET ROUGE at 10.15 pm. Any amount of kit for Coy can be taken on this limber. Above (or bags) to be at C.R. by 10 pm. The amount for Coy will accompany the limber.

6) Chargers. Coy Commders chargers will meet Coys at Town Majors Office VILLERS AU BOIS.

7) Stores. All Trench Stores except periscopes will be handed over to relieving Bn and a receipt obtained. Receipts to be handed in to O.R. on arrival at Estree.

8) Brigade School. Officers and O.R. now at Brigade School will rejoin Bn at ESTREE

Copy No 1 File.   (sgd) W B Twine
     "   2 140th Inf Bde   (Major)
     "   3 O.C. Coys   8th Lon Regt
     "   4 T.O & QMR   (p O.R.)
     "   5 140 T M B
     "   6 War Diary

"A" Form.
MESSAGES AND SIGNALS.
Army Form C. 2121.
No. of Message..........

Prefix... SP Code. ASA	Words 34	Charge	This message is on a/c of:	Recd. at 9·40 a.m.
Office of Origin and Service Instructions. PA Priority	Sent At .... m. To .... By		Service. (Signature of "Franking Officer.")	Date 7/7/16 From Oldfield A By

TO: **CANAD**

Sender's Number	Day of Month	In reply to Number	AAA
BM 175	7		

relief will take place tonight
as previously arranged aaa 0088
will therefore stand good
aaa Acknowledge aaa Addressed all
formations 140 inf Bde
repeated 140 inf Bde

From Place: CALAM
Time: 8·46 AM

282